Courtland L. Bovée / John V. T[...]

Professor of Business Communication
C. Allen Paul Distinguished Chair
Grossmont College

Chief Executive Officer
Communication Specialists of America

P9-DVF-481

BUSINESS COMMUNICATION TODAY

TEST ITEM FILE

SIXTH EDITION

Prentice Hall
Upper Saddle River, New Jersey 07458

Acquisitions editor: Linda Schreiber
Associate editor: Kristen Imperatore
Project editor: Richard Bretan
Manufacturer: Technical Communication Services

© 2000 by Prentice Hall, Inc.
Upper Saddle River, New Jersey 07458

Printed in the United States of America

10 9 8 7 6 5 4

ISBN 0-13-030044-6

Prentice-Hall International (UK) Limited, *London*
Prentice-Hall of Australia Pty. Limited, *Sydney*
Prentice-Hall Canada Inc., *Toronto*
Prentice-Hall Hispanoamericana, S.A., *Mexico*
Prentice-Hall of India Private Limited, *New Delhi*
Prentice-Hall of Japan, Inc., *Tokyo*
Prentice-Hall (Singapore) Pte Ltd
Editora Prentice-Hall do Brasil, Ltda., *Rio de Janeiro*

CONTENTS

PREFACE

Test Bank

This manual is organized by text chapters and includes a mix of multiple-choice, true-false, and fill-in questions for each chapter. Approximately 1,500 objective items have been carefully written and reviewed to provide a fair, structured program of evaluation. You can also get the complete test bank on computer disk.

Testing Services

Also available to adopters of *Business Communication Today* is *Prentice Hall Custom Test*, Windows version, which is based on a state-of-the-art test-generation-software program developed by Engineering Software Associates (ESA). *Prentice Hall Custom Test* can be customized to your class needs. You can create tests quickly, easily, and without error. You can generate an exam, you can administer it in the traditional fashion or online, and you can evaluate, track, and analyze student results.

CHAPTER 1
UNDERSTANDING BUSINESS COMMUNICATION

TRUE OR FALSE

F _____ 1. Communication and effective communication are basically the same thing. (p. 4)

T _____ 2. The most basic form of communication is nonverbal. (p. 4)

F _____ 3. Although nonverbal cues had significance in primitive times, they have little value in today's sophisticated world of communication. (p. 5)

F _____ 4. A person can learn to master the vocabulary of gestures, expressions, and inflections common in a culture by studying books on nonverbal communication. (p. 5)

F _____ 5. Businesspeople prefer written forms of communication to oral ones. (p. 5)

T _____ 6. People spend more time receiving information than transmitting it. (p. 6)

F _____ 7. Right after hearing a speech, we recall most, but not all, of what we heard. (p. 6)

F _____ 8. The information chain is limited to sources inside the organization. (p. 7)

T _____ 9. The more links in the formal communication chain, the greater the opportunity for distortion of messages. (p. 7)

T _____ 10. Most of the information that flows downward in an organization is geared toward helping employees do their jobs. (p. 9)

T _____ 11. Upward communication is just as important as downward communication. (p. 10)

F _____ 12. The danger of encouraging upward communication flow in an organization is that employees will report only the bad news. (p. 10)

F _____ 13. Horizontal communication occurs only through informal channels. (p. 10)

T _____ 14. The amount of horizontal communication that occurs through formal channels depends on the degree of interdependence among departments. (p. 10)

F _____ 15. The "grapevine" is another name for formal horizontal communication. (p. 10)

F _____ 16. Only 20 percent of the information that travels along the grapevine in an organization pertains to business. (p. 10)

T _____ 17. Instead of trying to eliminate the grapevine, sophisticated companies minimize its importance by making certain that the official word gets out. (p. 11)

1

T _____ 18.   External communication carries information in and out of the organization. (p. 11)

F _____ 19.   Since external communication is carefully orchestrated, almost none occurs informally. (p. 12)

F _____ 20.   Public relations and marketing functions are essentially the same. (p. 12)

F _____ 21.   The marketing department manages the company's reputation with such groups as employees, customers, and the general public. (pp. 12–13)

T _____ 22.   Communication tools commonly used by public relations departments include news releases, annual reports, letters, and speeches. (p. 14)

T _____ 23.   Experts recommend that companies designate a single spokesperson to handle requests for information during a crisis. (p. 14)

F _____ 24.   The way TWA handled public communications following the 1996 crash of Flight 800 should be used as a model for the best way to handle crisis communications. (p. 15)

T _____ 25.   Whether you're listening or speaking, communication is a two-way process. (p. 15)

T _____ 26.   A message is interpreted correctly when the receiver assigns to the words the same meaning as the sender intended and then responds in the desired way. (p. 16)

T _____ 27.   A major barrier to reception of messages is selective perception—focusing on the most relevant and general information. (p. 17)

T _____ 28.   The meaning of a word by itself is arbitrary, depending on a shared definition. (p. 17)

F _____ 29.   A person will usually react in the same way to the same words, no matter what the situation. (p. 17)

F _____ 30.   Differences in background present a barrier to communication that can be easily overcome. (p. 18)

F _____ 31.   Too much information is usually better than too little. (p. 20)

T _____ 32.   Filtering is screening out information before passing a message on to someone else. (p. 20)

T _____ 33.   The management style of top executives influences the organization's communication climate. (p. 20)

F _____ 34.   One way to foster an open communication climate in a company is to increase the number of levels in the organizational structure. (p. 21)

F _____ 35.   Feedback is easy to get, regardless of the transmission method you choose. (p. 22)

T _____ 36. If your audience doesn't understand your message, you should try to find the source of the misunderstanding and then revise your message. (p. 23)

F _____ 37. When people must choose between conflicting loyalties and weigh difficult trade-offs, they are facing an ethical lapse. (p. 23)

T _____ 38. Your ability to empathize with, be sensitive to, and generally consider your audience's feelings is the best way to be effective in your communication. (p. 26)

F _____ 39. The longer your message, the more points you should try to cover. (p. 28)

F _____ 40. "Media richness" refers to the prices various media are able to charge for their advertising. (p. 28)

MULTIPLE CHOICE

c _____ 1. The most basic form of communication is (p. 5)
　　　　a. the spoken word.
　　　　b. written symbols.
　　　　c. nonverbal communication.
　　　　d. grunting.

a _____ 2. Compared to nonverbal communication, verbal communication (p. 5)
　　　　a. is more structured.
　　　　b. is more spontaneous.
　　　　c. has more impact.
　　　　d. is more reliable.

c _____ 3. The aspect of communication that is relatively easy to control is your (p. 5)
　　　　a. facial expression.
　　　　b. vocal characteristics.
　　　　c. choice of words.
　　　　d. body language.

c _____ 4. Immediately after hearing a ten-minute speech, people typically tend to remember (p. 6)
　　　　a. almost all of it.
　　　　b. most of it.
　　　　c. about half of it.
　　　　d. very little of it.

a _____ 5. When managers depend on formal communication channels, they run the risk of (p. 7)
　　　　a. distortion.
　　　　b. giving employees too much information.
　　　　c. revealing too much.
　　　　d. getting too much feedback.

b _____ 6.   An example of downward communication flow is (p. 9)
  a. a junior staff person giving information to a staff supervisor.
  b. a sales manager giving instructions to a salesperson.
  c. an e-mail message about sick leave sent from one staff secretary to another.
  d. a company briefing held on the organization's top floor.

d _____ 7.   Formal methods for channeling information upward include (p. 10)
  a. group meetings.
  b. interviews with employees who are leaving the company.
  c. formal procedures for resolving grievances.
  d. all of the above.

c _____ 8.   The director of advertising writing a memo to the plant manager is an example of   (p. 10)
  a. upward communication flow.
  b. downward communication flow.
  c. horizontal communication flow.
  d. informal communication flow.

d _____ 9.   A casual conversation between co-workers is an example of (p. 10)
  a. upward communication flow.
  b. downward communication flow.
  c. interdepartmental communication flow.
  d. informal communication flow.

c _____ 10. How much of the information that travels along the grapevine actually pertains to business? (p. 10)
  a. almost none of it
  b. half of it
  c. more than three-quarters of it
  d. none of the above

d _____ 11. Some executives are wary of informal communication channels, possibly because they (p. 10)
  a. fear the spread of misinformation.
  b. believe only formal channels are efficient carriers of information.
  c. object to casual conversations on company time.
  d. fear a loss of their control over the flow of information.

b _____ 12. Because some of the information received through the grapevine is false or distorted, sophisticated companies try to (p. 11)
  a. eliminate the grapevine.
  b. minimize its importance.
  c. substitute new communication networks.
  d. punish all employees who hold casual conversations during work hours.

b _____ 13. The two organizational units that manage the flow of external messages are (p. 12)
  a. marketing and finance.
  b. marketing and public relations.
  c. public relations and benefits.
  d. finance and benefits.

a _____ 14. The typical marketing department is responsible, among other things, for (p. 12)
  a. customer service.
  b. billing.
  c. disseminating news about the company.
  d. production scheduling.

c _____ 15. One of the most visible functions of the PR department is (p. 14)
  a. preparing and distributing new product information.
  b. developing new markets.
  c. helping management plan for and handle crises.
  d. all of the above.

d _____ 16. Inept handling of a crisis may result in (p. 14)
  a. a severe drain on company finances.
  b. a grave blow to the company's reputation.
  c. a barrage of negative publicity.
  d. all of the above.

b _____ 17. In the first step of the communication process, (p. 15)
  a. the sender decides what to say.
  b. the sender has an idea.
  c. the sender chooses a medium of transmission.
  d. the sender transmits the message.

a _____ 18. You must take into account the message you want to convey, the location of your audience, the need for speed, and the formality of the situation when choosing (p. 16)
  a. a communication channel.
  b. a communication purpose.
  c. what to wear.
  d. gestures and facial expressions.

c _____ 19. The final link in the communication chain is (p. 16)
  a. sending the message.
  b. receiving the message.
  c. giving feedback to the sender.
  d. interpreting the message.

d _____ 20. Communication is effective only when (p. 16)
  a. the sender has a meaningful idea.
  b. the idea becomes a message.
  c. the message gets transmitted.
  d. each step of the communication process is successful.

c _____ 21. The most extreme example of how backgrounds can impede communication occurs when the communicators (p. 18)
  a. are different ages.
  b. are of different social status.
  c. come from different countries or cultures.
  d. have opposing political views.

b _____ 22.   Bad connections, poor acoustics, and illegible copy are all examples of (p. 18)
a.   problems with feedback.
b.   physical distractions.
c.   problems with background differences.
d.   overload problems.

d _____ 23.   On a typical day, the average white-collar worker sends and receives as many as
_____ messages. (p. 20)
a.   20
b.   70
c.   140
d.   190

b _____ 24.   Which of the following is *not* a principal quality of successful communicators? (p. 21)
a.   credibility
b.   aggression
c.   congeniality
d.   control

c _____ 25.   The term *corporate culture* refers to (p. 21)
a.   the number of organizational levels within a corporation.
b.   the extent to which corporations dominate a particular culture.
c.   the mixture of values, traditions, and habits that give a company its atmosphere or personality.
d.   a company's sponsorship of cultural events.

c _____ 26.   Which of the following characteristics contributes to effective organizational communication? (p. 23)
a.   a top-down management style
b.   unspoken limits on the kind of information that can be transmitted
c.   a commitment to ethical communication
d.   high salaries and good benefits

d _____ 27.   An organization can foster ethical behavior by (p. 25)
a.   helping top managers become more sensitive communicators.
b.   rewarding ethical actions.
c.   using ethics audits.
d.   doing all of the above.

b _____ 28.   The advantages of using an audience-centered approach include (pp. 25–26)
a.   the ability to ignore ethical questions completely.
b.   the ability to accomplish the other five factors that contribute to effective communication.
c.   the ability to get your own way, even if it isn't beneficial to your readers.
d.   all of the above.

a _____ 29. Of the following media, which is considered the richest? (p. 29)
   a. face-to-face communication
   b. e-mail
   c. memos
   d. letters

b _____ 30. One way to improve your business communication ability is to (p. 30)
   a. make sure you never fail.
   b. practice your skills as much as possible.
   c. use the telephone rather than write a memo.
   d. have extremely fast typists on staff.

FILL-INS

1. Collectively, the people with whom you interact—your colleagues, employees, supervisors, customers, and so on—are referred to as _____. (p. 4)

2. The exchange of information within an organization is referred to as _____ communication.. (p. 7)

3. A disadvantage of the formal communication change is that information may become _____ , so no one sees the big picture. (p. 8)

4. The informal communication network within an organization is referred to as the _____. (p. 10)

5. _____ _____ is closely related to marketing and is often confused with it, but the functions of the two differ. (p. 12)

6. One of the most important functions of the public relations department is to help management plan for and respond to _____ . (p. 14)

7. When you put your idea into a message that your receiver will understand, you are _____ the message. (p. 15)

8. Your receiver must cooperate by _____ your message—absorbing and understanding it. (p. 15)

9. After getting a message, a receiver responds by giving the sender _____ . (p. 15)

10. _____ is interference in the communication process that distorts or obscures the sender's meaning. (p. 17)

11. _____ is screening out or abbreviating information before a message is passed on to someone. (p. 20)

12. An organization's _____ _____ is the mixture of values, traditions, and habits that give a place its atmosphere or personality. (p. 21)

13. An ethical _____ involves choosing among conflicting alternatives that aren't clear-cut. (p. 23)

14. _____ _____ refers to the value of a medium in a given communication situation. (p. 28)

ANSWERS

1.	stakeholders	8.	decoding
2.	internal	9.	feedback
3.	fragmented	10.	noise
4.	grapevine	11.	filtering
5.	public relations	12.	corporate culture
6.	crises	13.	dilemma
7.	encoding	14.	Media richness

CHAPTER 2
LISTENING, WORKING IN TEAMS, AND
UNDERSTANDING NONVERBAL COMMUNICATION

TRUE OR FALSE

T _____ 1. People generally have more faith in nonverbal cues than they do in verbal messages. (p. 36)

F _____ 2. When you have a conscious purpose, you can often achieve it more economically with words than with gestures. (p. 36)

F _____ 3. In all cultures, maintaining eye contact is considered a sign of attention, interest, and courtesy. (p. 37)

T _____ 4. Your vocal characteristics reveal many things that you are unaware of but that have meaning for your audience. (p. 37)

F _____ 5. The one aspect of nonverbal communication that you have little or no control over is your physical attractiveness. (p. 37)

T _____ 6. In business situations, touching suggests dominance, so a higher-status person is more likely to touch a lower-status person than the other way around. (p. 37)

F _____ 7. One tip for improving your nonverbal communication skills is to smile as much as possible, whether you feel like smiling or not. (p. 39)

T _____ 8. One advantage of oral communication over written communication is that it satisfies people's need for human interaction. (p. 40)

T _____ 9. People are likely to judge the content of what you say by your appearance and delivery style. (p. 40)

F _____ 10. One of the main advantages of oral communication is that you don't need to plan what you're going to say or how you're going to say it. (p. 40)

F _____ 11. It is best to develop one speaking style and then apply it in all situations. (p. 40)

T _____ 12. Whatever speaking style you use, be sure to use the "you" attitude. (p. 40)

T _____ 13. Most people need to improve their listening skills. (p. 41)

T _____ 14. Most people prefer to talk rather than listen. (p. 41)

T _____ 15. The kinds of listening skills you use can vary from situation to situation. (p. 41)

F _____ 16. The goal of content listening is to evaluate the logic, validity, and implications of a message. (pp. 41–42)

F _____ 17. The goal of empathic listening is to solve the speaker's problem. (p. 42)

T _____ 18.   Defensiveness is a major barrier to effective listening. (p. 43)

F _____ 19. Most people are unable to process information as quickly as a speaker talks, so they get behind in comprehending what the speaker is saying. (p. 43)

T _____ 20. To listen more effectively, it helps to depersonalize the experience so that you decrease the emotional impact of what's being said. (p. 44)

F _____ 21. A good listener judges the speaker's delivery, not content. (p. 45)

F _____ 22. When giving feedback to a speaker, stick to general comments rather than specifics. (p. 45)

F _____ 23. A good listener judges the speaker's delivery, not content. (p. 45)

T _____ 24. Teams usually achieve greater performance levels than what would have been accomplished by the members working independently. (p. 45)

F _____ 25. Once a team has been formed and roles have been assigned, there is nothing to interfere with the group's accomplishing is goals. (p. 47)

T _____ 26. When making a decision, groups usually go through four phases: orientation, conflict, emergence, and reinforcement. (p. 48)

T _____ 27. The advantages of using group decision-making software are anonymity, honesty, and speed. (p. 48)

F _____ 28. In collaborative writing, the usual outcome is a document that is obviously written from many viewpoints. (p. 51)

F _____ 29. There is no such thing as an unproductive meeting. (p. 52)

F _____ 30. Informational meetings tend to be less predictable than decision-making meetings. (p. 52)

F _____ 31. If you are trying to solve a problem or make a decision, the more people in your group the better. (p. 52)

F _____ 32. A meeting agenda is just a guideline and doesn't really need to be adhered to. (p. 53)

F _____ 33. The main role of the meeting leader is to be passive and let others speak without interference. (p. 54)

F _____ 34. In this day and age, there is no need to follow parliamentary procedure in meetings. (p. 54)

F _____ 35. Conflict between persons or groups in an organization is destructive and must be avoided at all costs. (p. 55)

T _____ 36. To resolve conflict successfully, it helps to get feelings out in the open before dealing with the main issues. (p. 56)

T _____ 37. To resolve conflicts successfully, you seek reasons for the problems before seeking solutions. (p. 56)

T _____ 38. Typically, in a business situation, reason prevails. (p. 56)

F _____ 39. If you encounter irrational resistance, avoid calling the person's attention to it . (p. 56)

T _____ 40. Convincing someone of your viewpoint depends as much on the other person's frame of mind as it does on your arguments. (p. 57)

MULTIPLE CHOICE

b _____ 1. If a person says one thing but sends a conflicting message nonverbally, (p. 36)
   a. people are more likely to believe the verbal message.
   b. people are more likely to believe the nonverbal message.
   c. people are more likely to just stop listening.
   d. none of the above.

d _____ 2. Touching behavior (p. 37)
   a. is the least important form of nonverbal communication.
   b. is the great equalizer, putting people of different status on the same footing.
   c. should be completely avoided in all business situations.
   d. is governed by relatively strict customs that establish who can touch whom and when.

c _____ 3. To improve your nonverbal communication skills, it is a good idea to (p. 39)
   a. practice avoiding eye contact.
   b. learn how to smile at all times, no matter what your mood.
   c. learn how to avoid giving others conflicting signals.
   d. try your best to cover up your emotions.

d _____ 4. One of the major disadvantages of oral communication is that (pp. 39–40)
   a. people are able to interact with one another.
   b. it doesn't provide for feedback.
   c. it emphasizes verbal over nonverbal communication.
   d. people tend to confuse the message with the speaker.

a _____ 5. To be more effective in using speech as a tool for accomplishing your business objectives, you should (p. 40)
    a. break the habit of talking spontaneously without planning what you're going to say or how you're going to say it.
    b. take a class in public speaking.
    c. listen to good speakers and imitate them.
    d. learn how to manipulate people through using both verbal and nonverbal messages.

b _____ 6. When questioned about material they have just listened to, most people are likely to (p. 41)
    a. remember nearly all of the content correctly.
    b. get the facts mixed up.
    c. remember almost nothing.
    d. fake an answer.

a _____ 7. If you are listening mainly to understand and retain information imparted by a speaker, you are engaging in (p. 41)
    a. content listening.
    b. critical listening.
    c. empathic listening.
    d. active listening.

c _____ 8. If you are engaging in critical listening, your goal is to (p. 42)
    a. understand and retain information.
    b. understand the speaker's feelings, needs, and wants.
    c. evaluate the logic and validity of the message.
    d. appreciate the speaker's point of view.

c _____ 9. If you are listening mainly to understand the speaker's needs and wants, you are engaging in (p. 42)
    a. content listening.
    b. critical listening.
    c. empathic or active listening.
    d. sustained listening.

a _____ 10. The first step in the basic listening process is (p. 43)
    a. attending.
    b. interpreting.
    c. evaluating.
    d. responding.

d _____ 11. Self-centered listeners habitually (p. 43)
    a. take control of the conversation and tell you *their* problems.
    b. trivialize your concerns.
    c. emphasize their own knowledge of the topic.
    d. do all of the above.

b _____ 12. "Out-listening" refers to (p. 43)
   a. a highly focused form of listening.
   b. a form of selective listening in which the listener's mind wanders until something relevant is said.
   c. a form of defensive listening.
   d. listening only long enough to get a word in edgewise.

c _____ 13. To be a better listener (p. 44)
   a. tune out dry subjects.
   b. react to emotional words used by the speaker.
   c. listen for concepts and key ideas as well as facts.
   d. fake paying attention.

d _____ 14. When giving feedback, it is a good idea to (p. 45)
   a. be general rather than specific.
   b. be as personal in your comments as possible.
   c. focus on how the feedback can benefit you, personally.
   d. use "I" statements rather than "you" language.

a _____ 15. In participative management (p. 46)
   a. employees are involved in the company's decision making.
   b. all top-level managers participate in profit sharing.
   c. teams are discouraged in favor of individual achievement.
   d. an authoritarian management model is used.

b _____ 16. A hidden agenda refers to (p. 46)
   a. a meeting agenda that is not revealed to others outside the meeting group.
   b. individuals' private motives that affect a group's interaction.
   c. an agenda that members must look for before they can attend a meeting.
   d. an approach to group dynamics that helps facilitate group functioning.

c _____ 17. Group members who are motivated mainly to fulfill personal needs play a (p. 47)
   a. group-maintenance role.
   b. task-facilitating role.
   c. self-oriented role.
   d. coordinating role.

a _____ 18. Group members who try to help people work well together are able to fill a (p. 47)
   a. group-maintenance role.
   b. task-facilitating role.
   c. self-oriented role.
   d. coordinating role.

c _____ 19. Unwritten rules that govern the behavior of group members are referred to as (p. 47)
   a. group maintenance roles.
   b. parliamentary procedure.
   c. group norms.
   d. Robert's Rules.

a _____ 20. Groupthink refers to (p. 48)
  a. the willingness of individual group members to set aside their personal opinions and go along with everyone else.
  b. the four-step decision-making process in groups.
  c. software programs that help groups make decisions.
  d. the basic rules that underlie a group's behavior.

d _____ 21. During the reinforcement phase of group decision making, members (p. 48)
  a. socialize and establish roles.
  b. air all options and discuss their pros and cons.
  c. reach a decision.
  d. are given their assignments for carrying out the group's decision.

a _____ 22. An advantage of group decision-making software is (pp. 48–49)
  a. the anonymity of the participants.
  b. you don't need to be a good typist—just able to press buttons.
  c. everyone gets credit for the ideas they submit.
  d. it allows people to interact on a personal level.

c _____ 23. Working with other writers to produce a single document is called (p. 50)
  a. groupthink.
  b. participative management.
  c. collaborative writing.
  d. task facilitating.

a _____ 24. In collaborative writing, it is a good idea to (p. 51)
  a. designate one person to be the actual "author" of the document.
  b. begin by letting all members "do their own thing" and then seeing what they all produce.
  c. let all members use their own preferred software.
  d. establish a timeline and deadlines for every part of the project.

a _____ 25. In an informational meeting (p. 52)
  a. the participants share information and coordinate actions.
  b. the group must arrive at some kind of decision.
  c. brainstorming sessions are common.
  d. all of the above.

b _____ 26. A meeting agenda (p. 53)
  a. is a formality that most groups skip these days.
  b. should be circulated a few days before the meeting.
  c. should be general rather than specific.
  d. is only a guideline, and deviations are common and expected.

d _____ 27. When conducting a meeting (p. 54)
  a. if some people are too quiet, leave them alone; they probably have nothing to contribute.
  b. if some people dominate the conversation, let them do so, since they are probably the most knowledgeable attendees.
  c. try to simply act as an observer, and let the meeting "run itself."
  d. none of the above.

a _____ 28. For a win-win strategy to succeed, the parties must each accept that (p. 55)
     a. the other party can be trusted.
     b. the higher-status party has the only real option of imposing a solution in the long run.
     c. someone always has to win and someone always has to lose.
     d. competition is healthier than cooperation.

b _____ 29. A manager can transform a potentially disastrous conflict into an opportunity for creative change if he or she (p. 56)
     a. rigidly enforces the rules regardless of any possible fair solution.
     b. prevents the parties from becoming locked into their positions.
     c. avoids dealing with feelings and concentrates fully on facts.
     d. keeps the parties focused on one another and does not allow them to become distracted by "outside forces."

c _____ 30. The best way to handle an emotional reaction in a business setting is to (p. 56)
     a. let the party know that he or she is reacting emotionally.
     b. repeat yourself in hopes that this will help diffuse emotions.
     c. express understanding.
     d. agree with the other person's emotional reaction.

FILL-INS

1. When it comes to nonverbal communication, your _____ are especially effective for indicating attention and interest, regulating interaction, and establishing dominance. (p. 40)

2. The best way to earn other people's attention and goodwill is to remember the _____ attitude. (p. 40)

3. The goal of _____ listening is to evaluate the message at several levels. (p. 42)

4. The goal of _____ listening is to understand the speaker's feelings. (p. 42)

5. In the _____ stage of listening, you are decoding and absorbing what you hear. (p. 43)

6. You are engaging in _____ when you tune out a speaker until you hear a word or phrase that gets your attention once more. (p. 43)

7. Constructive criticism is a form of _____. (p. 45)

8. A _____ is a unit of two or more people who work together to achieve a goal. (p. 45)

9.   _____ _____ are the interactions and processes that take place in
      a meeting. (p. 46)

10.   Some group members have a _____ _____—private motives that
      affect the group's interaction. (p. 46)

11.   Group loyalty can lead members into _____, a willingness to set aside personal
      opinions and to go along with everyone else, even if everyone else is wrong. (p. 47)

12.   In _____ _____, a team of writers work together to produce a
      single document. (p. 50)

13.   When planning a meeting, the group leader prepares an _____ of items to discuss.
      (p. 53)

14.   The _____ strategy suggests that parties to a conflict can solve their problems better
      by working together rather than by waging war. (p. 55)

ANSWERS

1.	eyes	8.	team
2.	"you"	9.	group dynamics
3.	critical	10.	hidden agenda
4.	empathic	11.	groupthink
5.	interpreting	12.	collaborative writing
6.	out-listening	13.	agenda
7.	feedback	14.	win-win

CHAPTER 3
COMMUNICATING INTERCULTURALLY

TRUE OR FALSE

F _____ 1. International business communication has been hampered by tightening trade barriers throughout the world. (p. 62)

T _____ 2. Distinct groups that exist within a major culture are referred to as subcultures. (p. 62)

T _____ 3. Japan is an example of a country with a homogeneous population. (pp. 62–63)

T _____ 4. Cultural diversity is the degree to which a population is made up of people from various national, ethnic, racial, and religious backgrounds. (p. 64)

F _____ 5. Intercultural communication is the process of sending and receiving messages within a specific culture. (p. 65)

F _____ 6. The Puritan work ethic is a social value that's shared by nearly every culture in the world. (p. 65)

F _____ 7. A U.S. executive visiting the Middle East is correct to assume that a cramped and modest office indicates a lack of status. (p. 67)

F _____ 8. In China and Japan, important decisions are made by high-ranking executives and everyone else must abide by them. (p. 67)

F _____ 9. As global business heats up, everyone in business is aware how limited their time is, so it has become common for executives around the world to make every effort to get to the point quickly. (p. 67)

T _____ 10. People in Canada and the United States usually stand about five feet apart during a business conversation. (p. 68)

F _____ 11. Because the United States and Germany have such high-context cultures, they rely heavily on verbal communication and less on implied meaning. (p. 69)

T _____ 12. Differences in body language are a major source of misunderstanding in intercultural communication. (p. 69)

T _____ 13. In many parts of Latin America and Asia, keeping your eyes lowered is a sign of respect. (p. 69)

T _____ 14.   In Arab countries, it is impolite to take gifts to a man's wife, but it is acceptable to take gifts to his children. (p. 70)

F _____ 15.   When formal rules are violated, members of a culture find it difficult to explain why they feel upset. (p. 70)

T _____ 16.   From culture to culture, what people consider legal and ethical varies widely. (p. 70)

F _____ 17.   Regardless of the country you're doing business in, a person suspected of a crime is considered innocent until proven guilty. (p. 70)

T _____ 18.   Out of every seven people in the United States, one person speaks a language other than English when at home. (p. 71)

T _____ 19.   Even in an English-speaking country, language differences can trip you up, causing embarrassment if not costing profits. (p. 71)

T _____ 20.   Even when dealing with a businessperson who speaks your language, it's a mistake to assume that he or she understands everything you say. (p. 72)

T _____ 21.   Because Middle Easterners tend to speak more loudly than Westerners, they may be considered more emotional. (p. 72)

T _____ 22.   Many U.S.-based companies offer English language training programs for employees. (p. 73)

T _____ 23.   Ethnocentrism is the tendency to judge all other groups according to your own group's standards, behaviors, and customs. (p. 73)

F _____ 24.   By reacting ethnocentrically, you emphasize the distinctions between your own culture and another person's culture. (p. 73)

F _____ 25.   When ethnocentric people stereotype an entire group of people, they are usually justified in doing so. (p. 73)

T _____ 26.   Ethnocentric people fail to communicate with individuals as they really are. (p. 73)

T _____ 27.   Once you've acknowledged that cultural differences exist, the next step is to learn as much as possible about those cultures in which you plan to do business. (pp. 73–74)

F _____ 28.   When you're preparing to do business in another culture, even studying that culture in advance won't help you communicate more effectively. (p. 75)

F _____ 29.   If you don't have the time or the opportunity to learn a new language, your learning just a few words is considered insulting in most cultures. (p. 75)

F _____ 30.   A good way to gain favor with Arab businessmen is to offer them gifts of liquor. (p. 77)

T _____ 31.   To avoid the overgeneralization trap, learn useful general information while still being aware of and open to variations and individual differences. (pp. 77–78)

T _____ 32. You can communicate more effectively if you develop general skills that you can adapt in any culture. (p. 78)

F _____ 33. Surface culture consists of the attitudes and values on which a culture is based. (p. 79)

F _____ 34. Negotiators from the United States tend to be suspicious and distrusting of the other party. (p. 80)

T _____ 35. Chinese and Japanese negotiators seek to forge personal ties to establish long-term relationships before entering into serious negotiations.. (p. 80)

F _____ 36. Asian negotiators enjoy open conflict and a good debate. (p. 80)

T _____ 37. Materials most likely to need translation include advertisements, warranties, and product labels. (p. 80)

T _____ 38. In general, when writing to someone in another country, U.S. businesspeople should be a bit more formal than they would be otherwise. (pp. 80–81)

T _____ 39. When you speak English to someone for whom English is a second language, you should try to pronounce your words more clearly. (p. 83)

F _____ 40. If someone doesn't seem to understand you, your best response is to repeat the same words in a louder voice. (p. 83)

MULTIPLE CHOICE

d _____ 1. An example of an American subculture would be (pp. 62, 64)
  a. Cuban Americans.
  b. Grateful Dead fans.
  c. the Amish.
  d. all of the above.

b _____ 2. Cultural diversity is the degree to which the population is made up of people from various national, racial, religious, and (p. 64)
  a. economic backgrounds.
  b. ethnic backgrounds.
  c. employment backgrounds.
  d. ethical backgrounds.

b _____ 3. Many difficulties in intercultural communication occur because people in different cultures have different (p. 64)
  a. genetics.
  b. basic assumptions.
  c. environments.
  d. media.

c _____ 4.   By and large, people in the United States (p. 65)
                a.   value creating jobs more than working efficiently.
                b.   believe that people who work hard are no better than those who don't work hard.
                c.   dislike poverty and value hard work.
                d.   condemn materialism and prize a carefree lifestyle.

a _____ 5.   A spacious office, a big desk, and expensive accessories are most likely to be status
                symbols for executives in (p. 67)
                a.   the United States.
                b.   France
                c.   Saudi Arabia.
                d.   all of the above.

a _____ 6.   When it comes to decision-making customs, U.S. executives (p. 67)
                a.   try to reach decisions as quickly and as efficiently as possible.
                b.   prefer to make their deals slowly, after much discussion.
                c.   spend a lot of time on each little point to display their good faith.
                d.   arrive at decisions through consensus, after an elaborate and time-consuming process.

b _____ 7.   During a business conversation, U.S. and Canadian businesspeople usually stand (p. 68)
                a.   less than 12 inches apart.
                b.   about 5 feet apart.
                c.   about 8 feet apart.
                d.   more than 12 feet apart.

d _____ 8.   To convey meaning in a low-context culture such as the one existing in Germany, people rely
                more on (p. 69)
                a.   gestures and vocal inflection.
                b.   indirectness and metaphors.
                c.   situational cues.
                d.   explicit verbal communication.

b _____ 9.   When you violate informal rules of social behavior, the members of that culture (p. 70)
                a.   can usually explain why they feel upset.
                b.   may not be able to explain why they feel upset.
                c.   are unlikely to notice such an unimportant mistake.
                d.   will cheerfully correct your oversight and quickly forget the incident.

c _____ 10.   If a U.S.-based official pays a bribe to government officials in another country, it is
                (p. 70)
                a.   always considered a normal part of doing business.
                b.   considered unethical but not illegal to do so.
                c.   illegal, under the U.S. Foreign Corrupt Practices Act.
                d.   only unethical if the bribe is over $1,000.

d _____ 11.   A significant reason for the failure of alliances between U.S. companies and foreign ones is (p. 70)

    a.   monetary incompatibilities.

    b.   technological incompatibilities.

    c.   lack of ethics in the other countries.

    d.   culture clash.

a _____ 12.   After English, the language most commonly spoken in U.S. households is (p. 71)

    a.   Spanish.

    b.   French.

    c.   Japanese.

    d.   Italian.

b _____ 13.   Which of the following sentences contains an idiomatic expression? (p. 71)

    a.   Our product does not operate properly.

    b.   Our product doesn't cut the mustard.

    c.   Our product hasn't done as well as expected.

    d.   Our product could end up costing us dearly.

a _____ 14.   When you deal with people who don't speak your language at all, you have three options, including (p. 72)

    a.   using an intermediary or a translator.

    b.   using gestures and sign language.

    c.   speaking loudly and enunciating clearly.

    d.   using an English-only policy.

a _____ 15.   Japanese businesspeople tend to speak softly, a characteristic that to Western listeners implies (p. 72)

    a.   politeness or humility.

    b.   boredom or rudeness.

    c.   emotionalism.

    d.   all of the above.

a _____ 16.   Language and cultural barriers can be overcome by (p. 73)

    a.   maintaining an open mind.

    b.   judging other groups according to your own standards.

    c.   ignoring the distinctions between cultures.

    d.   remembering that people from other cultures communicate in ways that are inferior to your own.

a _____ 17.   When you react ethnocentrically, you (p. 73)

    a.   assume that others will act the same way you do.

    b.   recognize the differences that exist between your culture and other cultures.

    c.   focus on the possibility that your words and actions will be misunderstood.

    d.   do all of the above.

b _____ 18.   Stereotyping (p. 73)
             a.   is never a good practice.
             b.   can be useful in the early stages of learning about a culture.
             c.   lets you deal with individuals as they really are.
             d.   is often the result of thorough, specific, and accurate evidence.

c _____ 19.   Once you acknowledge that cultural differences exist, the next step is to (pp. 73–74)
             a.   learn how to interview and employ interpreters.
             b.   develop general skills for dealing with cultural diversity.
             c.   learn as much as possible about the cultures in which you plan to do business.
             d.   consider how to handle both written and oral communication.

b _____ 20.   If you don't have the time or the opportunity to learn a new language (p. 75)
             a.   make sure your colleagues abroad know yours.
             b.   learn at least a few words of your colleagues' language.
             c.   concentrate on your negotiating skills.
             d.   avoid face-to-face communication all together.

d _____ 21.   To learn as much as you can about a culture (p. 75)
             a.   read books and articles about the culture.
             b.   talk to people who have done business with members of that culture.
             c.   find out about the country's subcultures.
             d.   do all of the above.

a _____ 22.   Taking responsibility for communication means (p. 78)
             a.   not assuming it's the other person's job to communicate with you.
             b.   taking the initiative to greet new people in new situations.
             c.   admitting the mistakes you make when you communicate across differing cultures.
             d.   having the ability to blame the right person when communication breaks down.

b _____ 23.   Tolerating ambiguity means (p. 78)
             a.   learning to overlook such distractions as dress, appearance, and environmental discomfort.
             b.   learning to control your frustration when placed in an unfamiliar or confusing situation.
             c.   learning how best to pursue message meaning when communication is confusing and unclear.
             d.   all of the above.

c _____ 24.   Deep culture includes (p. 79)
             a.   holidays and celebrations.
             b.   fashions and styles.
             c.   attitudes and values.
             d.   all of the above.

a _____ 25.   Negotiators from France would most likely (p. 80)
             a.   favor an atmosphere of formal hospitality.
             b.   do anything to avoid open conflict.
             c.   take a long time to establish a personal relationship before beginning negotiations.
             d.   all of the above.

c _____ 26.   Negotiators from Japan would most likely (p. 80)
a.   enjoy confrontational, debate-oriented negotiations.
b.   remain distant and aloof.
c.   use a go-between or third party to assist in the negotiation.
d.   all of the above.

c _____ 27.   Many international documents are written in English and need no translation; however, some forms of written communication still need to be translated, including (p. 80)
a.   routine business correspondence.
b.   interoffice memos.
c.   advertisements, warranties, and procedure manuals.
d.   international business letters.

d _____ 28.   When writing letters to businesspeople in other countries, you should (p. 80)
a.   use an informal, friendly tone.
b.   keep your sentences and paragraphs long.
c.   be vague and general in your wording.
d.   make generous use of transitional words and phrases.

c _____ 29.   When dealing with someone from another culture, face-to-face communication (p. 83)
a.   puts your business relationship at risk.
b.   lets you avoid the much more difficult task of writing your message and saves you the expense of translation.
c.   lets you establish a personal relationship and gives you the benefit of immediate feed-back.
d.   wastes a lot of the time needed to run your business.

c _____ 30.   When speaking in English to people who use English as a second language (p. 83)
a.   forget about feedback; just make sure you get your message across.
b.   repeat your sentences often, a little louder each time.
c.   try to eliminate noise by pronouncing words clearly.
d.   use plenty of adjectives such as *fantastic* and *fabulous*.

FILL-INS

1.   _____ is a shared system of symbols, beliefs, attitudes, values, expectations, and norms for behavior. (p. 62)

2.   Groups that might be considered _____ in the United States are Mexican Americans, Mormons, and Russian immigrants. (pp. 62, 64)

3.   The degree to which a work force is made up of people from various national, ethnic, racial, and religious backgrounds reflects its _____ _____. (p. 64)

4.   The process of sending and receiving messages between people of different cultures is called _____ _____. (p. 65)

5. In a _____ culture such as exists in Taiwan, people rely less on verbal communication and more on the context of nonverbal actions and environmental setting to convey meaning. (p. 69)

6. In a _____ culture such as exists in Germany, people rely more on verbal communication and less on circumstances and implied meaning. (p. 69)

7. Differences in _____ _____, such as gestures and eye contact, are a major source of misunderstanding during intercultural communications. (p. 69)

8. Misunderstandings occur with language _____, which are word groupings that don't translate well literally. (p. 71)

9. One way to protect against poor translation is to _____ the same message into the original language. (p. 72)

10. If you react with _____, you tend to judge all other groups according to your own group's standards, behaviors, and customs. (p. 73)

11. Ethnocentric people are prone to _____, or attempting to predict individuals' behavior or character on the basis of their membership in a particular group. (p. 73)

12. Some experts say that culture exists on two levels, _____ culture and deep culture. (p. 79)

13. When you _____ with people from other cultures, you must learn about their problem-solving techniques, protocol, and decision-making methods. (p. 80)

14. When speaking to someone for whom English is a second language, you need to be particularly aware of _____ from the other person. (p. 83)

ANSWERS

1.	culture	8.	idioms
2.	subcultures	9.	back-translate
3.	cultural diversity	10.	ethnocentrism
4.	intercultural communication	11.	stereotyping
5.	high-context	12.	surface
6.	low-context	13.	negotiate
7.	body language	14.	feedback

CHAPTER 4
PLANNING AUDIENCE-CENTERED BUSINESS MESSAGES

TRUE OR FALSE

T _____ 1. The composition process includes three major phases: planning, organizing/composing, and revising. (p. 92)

F _____ 2. During the planning stage, you organize your message by preparing a preliminary outline. (p. 92)

F _____ 3. After you have planned, composed, and revised your message, you are ready to select the channel and medium for sending it. (p. 92)

F _____ 4. When allocating your time among the three stages of the composition process, you should use about a fourth of the time for planning, half the time for composing, and a quarter of the time for revising. (p. 93)

T _____ 5. Effective communicators complete all seven steps of the composition process, although not necessarily in exact order. (p. 93)

T _____ 6. Defining the purpose of your message helps you decide whether you should even proceed with composing the message. (p. 93)

T _____ 7. The three general purposes of business messages are to inform, to persuade, and to collaborate. (p. 93)

T _____ 8. If your message is intended strictly to inform, you control the message. (p. 94)

F _____ 9. If you seek to persuade your audience, you surrender all control over your message. (p. 94)

T _____ 10. Collaborative messages are high in audience participation but low in communicator control. (p. 94)

T _____ 11. Once you have established your purpose, it's best to consider whether it is worth pursuing at this time. (p. 94)

T _____ 12. There is no point in sending a message if its purpose isn't realistic. (p. 95)

F _____ 13. The best person to deliver a message is always the one who prepared it. (p. 95)

T _____ 14. No matter how you feel personally about a situation, your communication reflects your organization's priorities. (p. 95)

T _____ 15. When analyzing your audience, you should focus on the decision makers or opinion molders. (p. 96)

F _____ 16.   Large and small audiences behave in much the same ways. (p. 96)

T _____ 17.   If you are unsure of your audience's level of understanding, it is better to err on the side of providing too much information rather than running the risk of providing too little. (p. 97)

T _____ 18.   If you expect your audience to be skeptical, you will need to provide more proof and introduce your conclusions and recommendations more gradually. (p. 97)

T _____ 19.   The key to effective communication is to determine your audience's information needs and then respond to them. (p. 98)

F _____ 20.   When you get a vague request for information, the best way to handle it is to provide all the information you can and to allow audience members to pick and choose what is useful to them. (p. 98)

F _____ 21.   Good communicators include only the information that their audience has specifically requested. (p. 98)

T _____ 22.   It's always best to clearly state any action you want your audience to take, rather than beating around the bush or trying to be subtle. (p. 99)

F _____ 23.   Accuracy of information is less important in business communications than in other types of communication. (p. 99)

F _____ 24.   If you provide incorrect information in a business message, the best course of action is to say nothing and hope that no one notices. (p. 99)

F _____ 25.   Messages can be unethical simply because information is omitted. (p. 100)

T _____ 26.   In any kind of business communication, it's best to emphasize the points that you think will be especially interesting to your audience. (p. 100)

F _____ 27.   It is poor business practice to try to motivate your audience members to change their beliefs. (p. 100)

T _____ 28.   People are more likely to resist ideas that conflict with their existing beliefs and practices. (p. 100)

F _____ 29.   The "you" attitude refers to always keeping in mind how business communication will ultimately affect your career. (p. 102)

F _____ 30.   You cannot overdo the "you" attitude. (p. 102)

T _____ 31.   The "you" attitude should be avoided when assigning blame for a problem. (p. 103)

T _____ 32.   When someone makes a mistake, you should avoid dwelling on his or her failure and instead focus on how the person can improve. (p. 103)

F _____ 33.   Avoid using euphemisms because they are inherently dishonest. (p. 104)

F _____ 34.   Your audience's belief in your competence and integrity is not important; it's the content of your message that counts. (p. 104)

T _____ 35.   Being too modest can reduce your credibility with your audience. (p. 106)

F _____ 36.   In general, you need to use more tact and diplomacy in oral communication than in written communication. (p. 107)

F _____ 37.   It would be inappropriate to apply the term *actor* to a woman. (p. 108)

F _____ 38.   If you want to emphasize the confidentiality of a message, use a medium such as a fax or a memo. (p. 112)

T _____ 39.   The main advantage of written communication is that the writer has an opportunity to plan and control the message. (p. 114)

T _____ 40.   Electronic media are useful when you need speed, when you're physically separated from your audience, when you need to overcome time-zone barriers, and when you need to reach a dispersed audience personally. (p. 116)

MULTIPLE CHOICE

a _____ 1.   The three categories of steps involved in preparing a business message are (p. 92)
   a.   planning, composing, and revising.
   b.   informing, persuading, and collaborating.
   c.   defining the purpose, the main idea, and the topic.
   d.   satisfying the audience's informational, motivational, and practical needs.

c _____ 2.   The stage of the preparation process during which you step back to see whether you have expressed your ideas adequately is the (p. 92)
   a.   planning stage.
   b.   composing stage.
   c.   revising stage.
   d.   feedback stage.

d _____ 3.   You need a clear purpose for your message in order to (p. 93)
   a.   decide whether to proceed.
   b.   focus the content.
   c.   establish the channel and medium.
   d.   do all of the above.

c _____ 4.   Which of the following is *not* a general purpose common to business communication? (p. 93)
    a. to inform
    b. to persuade
    c. to negotiate
    d. to collaborate

b _____ 5.   The general purpose of a business message determines (p. 93)
    a. the gender of the speaker or writer.
    b. the amount of audience participation that is needed.
    c. the location of the audience.
    d. none of the above.

d _____ 6.   A message should be deferred or canceled if (p. 95)
    a. your news is bad.
    b. someone else wants to deliver it.
    c. your audience is highly receptive.
    d. the timing is wrong.

b _____ 7.   Audience analysis is relatively easy when you are communicating with (p. 95)
    a. strangers.
    b. your boss.
    c. large groups of people.
    d. customers on a mailing list.

b _____ 8.   The primary audience for your message is made up of (p. 96)
    a. all who receive it.
    b. the decision makers or opinion molders.
    c. those people with the highest status.
    d. those people who represent the opinions and attitudes of the majority.

c _____ 9.   When preparing a message for a large, diverse audience, you must (pp. 97-98)
    a. include as many visual aids as possible.
    b. solicit audience participation.
    c. look for the common denominators that tie the group together.
    d. do all of the above.

b _____ 10.   You need to provide more information in your message if (p. 97)
    a. you expect a favorable response.
    b. you are unsure about the audience's level of understanding.
    c. you and your audience share the same general background.
    d. all of the above are true.

d _____ 11.   If you face a skeptical audience, try to (p. 97)
    a. be as straightforward as possible about stating your conclusions and recommendations.
    b. avoid stating your conclusions and recommendations.
    c. use less evidence in support of your points.
    d. introduce your conclusions and recommendations gradually.

a _____ 12.   You need to determine what the audience wants to know, anticipate unstated questions, and emphasize ideas of greatest interest to your audience if you are to satisfy their (p. 98)
   a. information needs.
   b. motivational needs.
   c. emotional needs.
   d. practical needs.

c _____ 13.   A good way to test the thoroughness of your business message is to check it for (p. 98)
   a. a main idea.
   b. a purpose.
   c. the who, what, when, where, why, and how.
   d. accuracy.

c _____ 14.   If you make an honest mistake, such as giving incorrect information, the best thing to do is (p. 99)
   a. take no action.
   b. blame someone else.
   c. contact the primary audience immediately and correct the error.
   d. start looking for a new job.

a _____ 15.   When meeting your audience's informational needs, you emphasize ideas (p. 100)
   a. of greatest interest to the audience.
   b. that are uncontroversial.
   c. that will have the least impact on the audience.
   d. that don't need supporting evidence.

c _____ 16.   When people hear something that conflicts with their existing ideas, they (p. 100)
   a. usually remain open to what the communicator has to say.
   b. tend to pay more attention to the message.
   c. tend to resist the message.
   d. respond better to informative messages than to persuasive messages.

b _____ 17.   To overcome audience resistance, try to (p. 100)
   a. tell a few jokes to relax the audience.
   b. arrange your message so that the information will be as acceptable as possible.
   c. increase the amount of information in your message.
   d. decrease the amount of information in your message.

d _____ 18.   Which of the following statements best reflects the "you" attitude? (p. 102)
   a. "You failed to enclose a check for $25."
   b. "We need a check from you for $25 so that we can send the merchandise by May 15."
   c. "We will send you the merchandise as soon as we receive your check for $25."
   d. "You will have your merchandise by July 15 if you send us your check for $25 today."

b _____ 19.   It is best not to use the "you" attitude if (p. 103)
   a. you know your audience well.
   b. your organization prefers a more formal style.
   c. you are filling your audience's informational needs.
   d. you are preparing a persuasive message.

a _____ 20.   When you are criticizing or correcting, it is best to (p. 103)
a.   focus on what the person can do to improve.
b.   emphasize a person's mistakes so that he or she will not make the same mistakes again.
c.   call a spade a spade and call attention to the person's failures or shortcomings.
d.   make the person an example for everyone else to learn from.

c _____ 21.   The best approach to getting someone to buy a magazine subscription from your charity group would be to say (p. 104)
a.   "Please buy a subscription; our group really needs the money."
b.   "If you buy a subscription from me I'll make my quota."
c.   "This magazine will keep you informed on issues that affect your daily life."
d.   "Our group doesn't get any assistance from government agencies, so these magazine sales are our main source of funding."

d _____ 22.   A euphemism is a word or phrase that is (p. 104)
a.   possibly offensive.
b.   general or abstract in meaning.
c.   highly technical.
d.   a milder term for one with negative connotations.

c _____ 23.   To communicate credibility to your audience, you (p. 106)
a.   impress them with a long list of your accomplishments.
b.   are modest and deferential.
c.   show that you are confident and that you believe in yourself and in your message.
d.   use hedge words ("maybe," "perhaps") to demonstrate your knowledge that no issue is fully cut and dried.

c _____ 24.   You earn respect from your audience by (p. 107)
a.   being brutally frank in your criticisms.
b.   flattering them as much as possible.
c.   being polite and diplomatic.
d.   all of the above.

d _____ 25.   Instead of using the generic pronoun *he,* rephrase your sentence by (p. 108)
a.   using *he or she.*
b.   recasting it in the plural.
c.   eliminating the need for a pronoun.
d.   all of the above.

b _____ 26.   Which of the following is *not* a preferred way to refer to people? (pp. 108–109)
a.   "Ms. Smith is chair of the event."
b.   "The dignitaries at the event included Phil Donahue and his wife, Marlo."
c.   "Ms. Martinez and Mr. Wong are salespersons with the company."
d.   "Nicole Kidman is one of my favorite actors."

d _____ 27.   Which of the following sentences is the most preferable? (p. 109)
   a.   "Now in her fifties, Ms. Feldman can still cut a rug."
   b.   "Despite her WASP background, Ms. Feldman shows plenty of rhythm."
   c.   "Even though she suffers from epilepsy, Ms. Feldman has no problem out on the dance floor."
   d.   "Ms. Feldman is an excellent dancer."

d _____ 28.   The chief advantage of oral communication is (p. 112)
   a.   the ability to plan and control the message.
   b.   the opportunity to meet an audience's information needs.
   c.   the ability to transmit highly complex messages.
   d.   the opportunity for immediate feedback.

b _____ 29.   A written message is preferable to an oral one when (p. 114)
   a.   immediate feedback is desired.
   b.   the audience is large and geographically dispersed.
   c.   the message is relatively simple.
   d.   the information is controversial.

b _____ 30.   If you need to send a short, unambiguous message, the best electronic medium is (p. 116)
   a.   videoconferencing.
   b.   voice mail.
   c.   videotape.
   d.   CD-ROM.

FILL-INS

1.   During the _____ stage of the composition process, you define your purpose, analyze your audience, and select the channel and medium for the message. (p. 92)

2.   The first step in the planning phase is to define your _____. (p. 93)

3.   The three general purposes of business messages are to inform, to persuade, or to _____ with the audience. (p. 93)

4.   During the planning phase you also need to analyze your _____, including its size and composition, existing knowledge about the subject, and probable reaction to your message. (p. 95)

5.   As a communicator, you need to satisfy your audience's _____, motivational, and practical needs. (p. 98)

6.   As your company's representative, you have an obligation to be sure that all the information you provide is _____. (p. 99)

7. Using a _____ attitude allows you to establish empathy with your audience. (p. 102)

8. Instead of using harsh, unpleasant terms, use mild words, or _____. (p. 104)

9. If your audience is unfamiliar with you, you need to devote the initial part of your message to establishing _____. (p. 104)

10. To avoid embarrassing blunders in language related to gender, race, ethnicity, age or disability, use _____ language. (p. 107)

11. When you communicate with people outside your organization, you need to be sure to project the right _____ for your company. (p. 110)

12. Factors you should consider in choosing a communication channel and _____ include formality, confidentiality, feedback, time, and cost. (p. 112)

13. Telephone calls, meetings, videoconferences, and speeches are all types of _____ communication. (p. 112)

14. A standard paragraph that can be selected to suit a particular occasion or audience is called a _____. (p. 114)

ANSWERS

1.	planning	8.	euphemisms
2.	purpose	9.	credibility
3.	collaborate	10.	bias-free
4.	audience	11.	image
5.	informational	12.	medium
6.	accurate	13.	oral
7.	"you"	14.	boilerplate

CHAPTER 5
ORGANIZING AND COMPOSING
AUDIENCE-CENTERED BUSINESS MESSAGES

TRUE OR FALSE

F _____ 1. The purpose of a well-organized message is to get the audience to read everything, not just look for the specific information they need. (p. 125)

T _____ 2. Top executives consider clear, well-organized writing to be an indication of the writer's clear thinking. (p. 127)

F _____ 3. A well-organized message tends to be longer than a disorganized one. (p. 127)

F _____ 4. Good organization is a two-step process: First you define and group the ideas; then you write your introduction and conclusion. (p. 128)

T _____ 5. Every business message can be boiled down to one main idea. (p. 129)

F _____ 6. A message's topic, purpose, and main idea are virtually identical. (p. 129)

T _____ 7. When you must present disappointing or unwelcome information, it's best to choose a main idea that will establish a good relationship between you and your audience. (p. 130)

T _____ 8. A good brainstorming technique to use for establishing an informative message's main idea is the journalistic approach. (p. 132)

T _____ 9. You can keep your message brief if you are presenting routine information to a knowledge-able audience that already finds you credible. (p. 132)

F _____ 10. The longer your message, the more major points you cover. (p. 132)

T _____ 11. When you are preparing a long and complex message, an outline is indispensable. (p. 133)

F _____ 12. The only way to plan a business message is to use a formal alphanumeric outline. (p. 133)

F _____ 13. Even if your subject is routine and the audience is positively inclined toward your message, you need to include a lot of facts and figures to demonstrate your points. (p. 134)

F _____ 14. When providing supporting evidence for points you are making, stick to one type of detail (facts and figures, illustrations, or descriptions) because mixing types of evidence may confuse your readers. (p. 135)

F _____ 15. In the direct approach, the evidence comes first, and the main idea comes later. (p. 136)

F _____ 16.   The direct approach is used for short messages, such as memos and letters; the indirect approach is used for long messages, such as reports and proposals. (p. 136)

T _____ 17.   Routine messages call for the direct approach. (p. 136)

F _____ 18.   The most persuasive messages are those that take the direct approach. (p. 139)

F _____ 19.   Once you prepare your outline, you shouldn't deviate from it when writing the draft. (p. 139)

F _____ 20.   When preparing your first draft, you are not concerned about style or tone. (p. 139)

F _____ 21.   Good business letters use language that is as formal as possible and use proven terminology such as "please be advised that" and "we are in receipt of." (p. 140)

F _____ 22.   Enlivening business messages with humor will always please your readers, especially if they don't know you very well. (p. 141)

T _____ 23.   Bragging about your company's accomplishments can be offensive to readers. (p. 141)

F _____ 24.   Plain English is a style of writing used primarily for communicating to those for whom English is a second language. (p. 139)

T _____ 25.   Choosing the most effective words for a message is usually more difficult than merely choosing correct words. (p. 143)

F _____ 26.   Conjunctions, prepositions, articles, and pronouns are all content words. (p. 143)

F _____ 27.   Connotative meanings are the literal or dictionary meanings of words. (p. 144)

T _____ 28.   In business communication you must be careful to use words that are low in connotative meaning. (p. 145)

F _____ 29.   Abstract words are direct, vivid, clear, and exact. (p. 146)

F _____ 30.   Abstract words should be completely avoided in business writing. (p. 146)

F _____ 31.   A compound sentence is one that contains one main thought (independent clause) and one or more subordinate thoughts (dependent clauses). (p. 148)

F _____ 32.   Good business messages contain few compound or complex sentences. (p. 148)

T _____ 33.   Passive verbs make sentences longer and de-emphasize the subject. (p. 149)

T _____ 34.   Most business writing has an average sentence length of 20 words or fewer. (p. 150)

F _____ 35.   In business writing, the topic sentence of each paragraph is usually implied rather than explicit. (p. 151)

T _____ 36. Coherence within and between paragraphs is achieved through the use of transitional words and phrases. (p. 152)

F _____ 37. When developing paragraphs, stick to one method within each paragraph and throughout a document. (p. 152)

F _____ 38. Each paragraph in a business message revolves around four or five general ideas. (p. 154)

T _____ 39. Organization and style are as important for e-mail as for other kinds of messages. (p. 155)

F _____ 40. Spelling and grammar are less important in e-mail messages than in other kinds of business messages, since e-mail messages are more informal. (p. 156)

MULTIPLE CHOICE

b _____ 1. Which of the following is *not* one of the common faults responsible for most of the organizational problems in business messages? (pp. 124–126)
   a. The writer includes irrelevant material.
   b. The writer gets to the point too soon.
   c. The writer presents ideas in illogical order.
   d. The writer leaves out necessary information.

c _____ 2. Which of the following is *not* one of the benefits of a well-organized message? (pp. 125–127)
   a. It makes the message more acceptable to the audience.
   b. It saves the audience's time.
   c. It ensures that the audience will agree with the message.
   d. It helps the audience understand the message.

b _____ 3. Eliminating superfluous information from your message will (p. 127)
   a. result in a dry, boring message.
   b. save the audience's time.
   c. make the message seem incomplete.
   d. do all of the above.

a _____ 4. The main idea of a message is (p. 129)
   a. the "hook" that sums up why a particular audience should do or think as you suggest.
   b. the broad subject of a message.
   c. identical with the topic.
   d. all of the above.

c _____ 5. Which of the following is an example of a message topic? (p. 129)
   a. "To get the board of directors to increase the research and development budget"
   b. "Competitors spend more than our company does on research and development"
   c. "Funding for research and development"
   d. "The research and development budget is inadequate in our competitive marketplace"

c _____ 6. When you use an FCR worksheet, you're using a technique of brainstorming that involves (p. 131)
   a. consulting your friends, colleagues, and in-house reports.
   b. making a list of everything that pops into your head as you think about your message.
   c. visualizing the relationships among your findings, your conclusions, and your recommendations.
   d. assigning columns and numbers to a group of questions and answers related to your message in order to rank their importance.

a _____ 7. The number of major points in your message (p. 132)
   a. is three or four, regardless of how long the message is.
   b. is three for short messages, four or five for medium-length messages, and six or seven for longer messages.
   c. depends on whether the message is oral or written.
   d. can be unlimited if your audience is knowledgeable about the topic.

a _____ 8. When preparing an "organization chart" to help organize a message, you begin with (p. 133)
   a. the main idea.
   b. the major points.
   c. supporting evidence.
   d. whatever you want to begin with.

b _____ 9. Everything in a well-written business message (p. 133)
   a. is included in the outline.
   b. either supports the main idea or explains its implications.
   c. is entertaining.
   d. does all of the above.

c _____ 10. The specific evidence included in a business message should be (pp. 134–135)
   a. as abstract as possible.
   b. minimal if your subject is complex or unfamiliar.
   c. enough to be convincing but not so much that it's boring.
   d. all of the same type, such as examples or statistics.

c _____ 11. It is better to use the indirect approach if your audience will (p. 136)
   a. have a positive reaction.
   b. be neutral about what you have to say.
   c. be displeased by what you have to say.
   d. be above you in the hierarchy.

a _____ 12. It is preferable to use the direct approach with (p. 136)
   a. routine, good-news, and goodwill messages.
   b. bad-news messages.
   c. persuasive messages.
   d. all of the above.

b _____ 13. When you have bad news to convey, it's a good idea to (p. 138)
   a. put the bad news at the beginning of your message, thus getting it out of the way immediately.
   b. begin with a neutral statement that leads to the bad news gradually.
   c. put the bad news at the very end of your message.
   d. put off communicating the bad news in hopes the person will get the bad news from someone else.

c _____ 14. For persuasive messages, the best approach is to (p. 139)
   a. be honest yet kind.
   b. get straight to the point.
   c. begin by making an interesting point that will capture the audience's attention.
   d. open with the main idea and then provide supporting points.

b _____ 15. Which of the following sentences contains the strongest and most effective wording? (p. 140)
   a. "Given the parameters of the situation, the most propitious choice would be to make adjustments in certain budget areas."
   b. "We need to cut the operating budget by 12 percent or profits will plummet."
   c. "Someone's going to need to do some budget cutting around here or heads will roll."
   d. "Perusal of budgetary figures reveals that a 12 percent reduction in operations is called for if we are to stave off a negative impact on profits."

c _____ 16. Which of the following is *not* an example of pompous language? (p. 140)
   a. "as per your letter"
   b. "please be advised that"
   c. "please let us know"
   d. "under separate cover"

b _____ 17. Plain English is a style of writing (p. 142)
   a. used only for casual correspondence.
   b. designed to make technical materials more understandable to the audience.
   c. aimed primarily at readers for whom Engish is a second language.
   d. inappropriate for business communication.

a _____ 18. Which of the following are functional words? (p. 143)
   a. into, and, the
   b. bath, baby, rattle
   c. give, shake, wash
   d. nice, wet, quickly

c _____ 19. Which of the following is a content word? (p. 143)
   a. around
   b. she
   c. jump
   d. the

c _____ 20. The connotative meaning of a word is (pp. 144–145)
    a. its dictionary meaning.
    b. its literal meaning.
    c. all the associations and feelings the word evokes.
    d. its objective meaning.

d _____ 21. Which of the following words are the most abstract? (pp. 145–146)
    a. kiss, rose, house
    b. red, sharp, piercing
    c. kick, sniff, tickle
    d. love, beauty, innocence

a _____ 22. Which of the following is a compound sentence? (p. 148)
    a. "David is a good worker, and he deserves a raise."
    b. "Because David is a good worker, he deserves a raise."
    c. "David, a good worker, deserves a raise."
    d. "Having been a good worker, David will no doubt receive a raise."

d _____ 23. A complex sentence is one characterized by (p. 148)
    a. two independent clauses joined by a coordinating conjunction.
    b. a single subject and a single predicate plus any modifying phrases.
    c. two or more independent clauses along with all modifying phrases.
    d. an independent clause and one or more dependent clauses related to it.

c _____ 24. To downplay a dependent clause in a complex sentence, you (p. 148)
    a. place it at the beginning of the sentence.
    b. place it at the end of the sentence.
    c. bury it in the middle of the sentence.
    d. set it off with a semicolon.

a _____ 25. Using the passive voice makes sense when (p. 148)
    a. you want to be diplomatic in pointing out a problem or error.
    b. you want your sentence to be easier to understand.
    c. you need to make your sentences shorter.
    d. you want to emphasize the subject.

a _____ 26. Short sentences are best for (p. 150)
    a. emphasizing important information.
    b. grouping or combining ideas.
    c. showing relationships among ideas.
    d. summarizing or previewing information.

a _____ 27. A typical paragraph contains the three basic elements of (p. 151)
    a. a topic sentence, related sentences, and transitional elements.
    b. simple, compound, and complex sentences.
    c. the main idea, supporting ideas, and evidence.
    d. a problem, discussion, and a solution.

d _____ 28. Words such as "nevertheless," "however," "but," and "therefore" (p. 152)
  a. are called pointer words.
  b. introduce modifiers.
  c. occur only in complex sentences.
  d. are useful for making transitions.

b _____ 29. A paragraph developed by cause and effect (p. 153)
  a. points out similarities or differences between ideas.
  b. gives the reasons for something.
  c. gives examples that illustrate the general idea.
  d. shows how a general idea is broken into specific categories.

d _____ 30. How is the following paragraph developed?
  "Improving our performance will be difficult this year, given the slowdown in the economy. However, even though sales are relatively flat, profits can be improved if we trim costs. The two most promising targets for improvement are direct labor costs and overhead, because analysis of industry data suggests we are above the average in both these categories." (p. 153)
  a. by comparison
  b. by classification
  c. by illustration
  d. by discussion of problem and solution

FILL-INS

1. The central point or theme of a message is its _____ _____.
    (p. 129)

2. The storyteller's tour, FCR worksheet, and question-and-answer chain are all methods of
    _____. (p. 139)

3. In the _____ approach to organizing a message, the main idea comes first, followed
    by the evidence. (p. 136)

4. In the _____ approach to organizing a message, the evidence comes first, and the
    main idea comes later. (p. 136)

5. *Style* is the way you use words to achieve a certain _____, or overall impression. (p. 139)

6. _____ words express relationships and have only one unchanging meaning in any
    given context; _____ words, such as nouns, verbs, adjectives, and adverbs, carry the
    meaning of the sentence. (p. 143)

7.   The _____ meaning of a word is its literal, dictionary meaning, whereas the _____ meaning includes all the associations and feelings it evokes. (p. 144)

8.   A(n) _____ word expresses a concept or quality, not a tangible object. (p. 145)

9.   A _____ sentence expresses two or more independent but related thoughts of equal importance. (p. 148)

10. A _____ sentence expresses one main thought and one or more subordinate thoughts related to it. (p. 148)

11. A sentence is _____ when the subject follows the verb and the object precedes it. (p. 149)

12. A _____ is a cluster of sentences related to the same general topic. (p. 151)

13. Most paragraphs consist of a _____ sentence, related sentences, and transitional elements. (p. 151)

14. Coherence is achieved through the use of _____ that show the relationship between paragraphs and among sentences within paragraphs. (p. 152)

ANSWERS

1.   main idea
2.   brainstorming
3.   direct (deductive)
4.   indirect (inductive)
5.   tone
6.   functional, content
7.   denotative, connotative

8.   abstract
9.   compound
10. complex
11. passive
12. paragraph
13. topic
14. transitions

CHAPTER 6
REVISING AUDIENCE-CENTERED BUSINESS MESSAGES

TRUE OR FALSE

T _____ 1. When revising a business message, you should try to go through your document three times: once for content and organization, once for style and readability, and once for mechanics and format. (p. 164)

T _____ 2. Editing is an ongoing activity that occurs throughout the composition process. (p. 164)

T _____ 3. It is a good idea to set aside a first draft for a day or two before beginning the revision process. (p. 164)

F _____ 4. The middle section of a message has the greatest impact on the audience. (p. 164)

F _____ 5. The most common readability formulas measure the number of letters in all the words of a sample paragraph to give you a rough idea of the level of your material. (p. 167)

T _____ 6. Although readability formulas are easy to apply, they ignore some factors that contribute to reading ease. (p. 168)

F _____ 7. Most good communicators get their message right the first time and don't need to worry about rewriting. (p. 168)

F _____ 8. A major complaint among business executives is that most of the written messages they receive are too short. (p. 169)

T _____ 9. The word *very* is usually unnecessary and contributes to sentence clutter. (p. 169)

T _____ 10. Short words are more vivid and easier to read than long words. (p. 170)

F _____ 11. Redundancies are useful to readers because repetition leads to better recall of information. (p. 170)

T _____ 12. "Consensus of opinion," "at the present time," and "until such time as" are all examples of expressions that could be replaced with single words. (p. 170)

T _____ 13. If you start a sentence with an indefinite pronoun, chances are the sentence can be shortened. (p. 170)

F _____ 14 To save words, make liberal use of such directional points as "the latter," "the former," "the aforementioned," and "as mentioned above." (p. 171)

F _____ 15.   Your writing will be more impressive if you string together several short sentences into one long one. (p. 171)

F _____ 16.   To avoid making a judgment in your business messages, you should use as many hedging words (such as *may* or *seems*) as possible. (p. 171)

T _____ 17.   Parallel construction makes sentences more readable. (p. 172)

T _____ 18.   Dangling modifiers are often the result of passive constructions. (p. 173)

T _____ 19.   A camouflaged verb is a verb that has been turned into a noun or an adjective. (p. 173)

T _____ 20.   The subject and predicate of a sentence should be kept as close together as possible. (p. 174)

T _____ 21.   When critiquing someone else's writing, you should try to make your comments as constructive as possible. (p. 175)

F _____ 22.   A document should not be released or published until it is absolutely perfect, even it that means missing a deadline. (p. 176)

T _____ 23.   Groupware is software that allows many people to compose and edit a single document at the same time from different locations. (p. 176)

F _____ 24.   Readers expect business documents to have a certain number of mistakes and typos and tend to ignore any that they encounter. (p. 177)

F _____ 25.   Word-processing software is no longer the dominant tool for creating printed documents. (p. 177)

F _____ 26.   The only way to enter text into your computer is to type it in on a keyboard. (p. 178)

T _____ 27.   With some computers, you don't have to type at all. (pp. 178–179)

T _____ 28.   A boilerplate is any standard block of text used in various documents without change. (p. 180)

F _____ 29.   When you want to separate one computer file into four separate files, you use a word-processing capability known as *file merge*. (p. 179)

T _____ 30.   Technology makes it possible to "doctor" photos, a practice that raises ethical and legal questions. (p. 180)

F _____ 31.   The term *cut and paste* is used in both word processing and desktop publishing and refers to the ability to track down selected words and phrases and replace or delete them. (p. 180)

F _____ 32.   Spell checkers are the only tool you need to guarantee error-free documents. (p. 181–182)

F _____ 33.   Because computers have become so powerful, grammar checkers can easily determine whether your document states your message correctly and communicates it clearly. (p. 182)

F _____ 34. For all the technological advances in communication, there is still no way of attaching a spoken message or other sound to particular places in a document. (p. 183)

T _____ 35. Style sheets can help ensure that every section of a document is formatted consistently. (p. 186)

T _____ 36. Word-processing software can keep track of your footnotes and renumber all f them every time you add or delete references. (p. 186)

T _____ 37. You should avoid centering long blocks of type. (p. 187)

F _____ 38. Sans serif typefaces are preferable to serif typefaces when designing long blocks of text. (p. 187)

F _____ 39. Using as many different typefaces as possible makes your business documents more appealing. (p. 188)

T _____ 40. Sending messages via fax is indispensable for international business communication. (p. 189)

MULTIPLE CHOICE

c _____ 1. When editing for content and organization, pay special attention to (p. 164)
  a. grammar and usage.
  b. punctuation and spelling.
  c. the beginning and ending of the message.
  d. style and tone.

a _____ 2. One of the best-known readability formulas is the (p. 167)
  a. Fog Index.
  b. 2 +2 formula.
  c. scan plan.
  d. Carnegie Index.

c _____ 3. For general business messages, your writing should be geared to readers at the (p. 168)
  a. first- to fourth-grade level.
  b. fifth- to sixth-grade level.
  c. eighth- to eleventh-grade level.
  d. twelfth- to fourteenth-grade level.

d _____ 4. Which of the following sentences is the most concisely worded without being ambiguous? (pp. 169–170)
  a. The project manager is in charge of specifications until such time as the project gets underway."
  b. The project manager should provide specifications prior to the start of a project."
  c. Project managers have the capability of changing specifications."
  d. The project managers told the engineers last week that the specifications were changed."

b _____ 5. "Surrounded on all sides" is an example of (p. 170)
    a. a cliché.
    b. redundancy.
    c. the passive voice.
    d. obsolete language.

a _____ 6. Starting a sentence with "It" or "There" is (p. 170)
    a. using an indefinite pronoun starter.
    b. perfectly acceptable, and you need not try to rewrite the sentence.
    c. a sign of the active voice being used.
    d. all of the above.

d _____ 7. "The above-mentioned book" is an example of (p. 171)
    a. a redundancy.
    b. a strung-out sentence.
    c. an indefinite pronoun starter.
    d. an awkward pointer.

b _____ 8. "The deadline for getting taxes filed is two weeks away, and you need to talk to your accountant soon" is an example of (pp. 171–172)
    a. a redundancy.
    b. a strung-out sentence.
    c. an indefinite pronoun starter.
    d. an awkward pointer.

a _____ 9. What is wrong with the following sentence? "We plan to launch the new plastics line in France, England, Germany, and in Sweden in 1992." (pp. 172–173)
    a. Items in a series are not parallel.
    b. It contains a dangling modifier.
    c. It contains a split infinitive.
    d. It is grammatically correct as written.

b _____ 10. What is wrong with the following sentence? "Driving to the office, a police officer stopped me for speeding." (p. 173)
    a. It lacks parallelism.
    b. It contains a dangling modifier.
    c. It contains an awkward pointer.
    d. It is grammatically correct as written.

d _____ 11. "Government task force report recommendations" is an example of (p. 173)
    a. redundancy.
    b. a dangling modifier.
    c. a dependent clause.
    d. stringing together a series of nouns.

c _____ 12. Which of the following sentences contains a camouflaged verb? (p. 173)
    a. "Some do; others don't."
    b. "She is a marketing manager but also serves as ad manager."
    c. "It is John's recommendation that she be hired."
    d. "He slowly, deliberately added the numbers."

b _____ 13. When critiquing someone else's writing, which of the following is *not* an element you should concentrate on? (p. 175)
  a. Does the document accomplish its intended purpose?
  b. Does it fit your personal preferences?
  c. Is the factual material correct?
  d. Is the language unambiguous?

a _____ 14. The tool that lets you write with an electronic stylus on a special pad (which converts your handwriting to text the computer can recognize) is called a (p. 178)
  a. pen-based computer.
  b. dictation system.
  c. scanner.
  d. grammar checker.

b _____ 15. A boilerplate is (p. 179)
  a. a type of computer software used to help sort files.
  b. a standard block of text that can be used in various documents without being changed.
  c. an unethical means for plagiarizing the work of others.
  d. a cumbersome, time-consuming series of actions required by some word processors.

c _____ 16. Your word processor's file merge capability allows you to (p. 179)
  a. proofread your printed document.
  b. store innumerable facts, from financial figures to texts of reports.
  c. combine numerous documents into one.
  d. do none of the above.

d _____ 17. Scanning technologies raise ethical questions because they allow you to (p. 180)
  a. retouch photos as you see fit.
  b. make products and people look better or worse than they really do.
  c. create situations that don't really exist.
  d. do all of the above.

a _____ 18. Word-processing software helps you revise documents through the use of (p. 180)
  a. the search and replace function.
  b. the outlining function.
  c. the database function.
  d. all of the above.

d _____ 19. A spell checker (p. 181)
  a. compares your document with an electronic dictionary.
  b. highlights words it doesn't recognize.
  c. suggests correct spelling.
  d. does all of the above.

b _____ 20. A grammar checker (p. 182)
  a. scans visual images into your computer.
  b. highlights phrases in passive voice.
  c. suggests correct spelling.
  d. helps you find just the right word for a given situation.

c _____ 21.   A grammar checker cannot tell (p. 182)
     a.   the difference between passive and active voice.
     b.   whether a sentence is long or short.
     c.   whether your document communicates clearly.
     d.   any of the above.

b _____ 22.   To hear spoken messages or other sounds attached to a document, receivers must (p. 183)
     a.   convert the document to tape and use a tape player.
     b.   load the document into a computer.
     c.   insert the document into an optical character recognition system.
     d.   receive the document over a phone line.

a _____ 23.   Inserting hypertext into documents (p. 183)
     a.   involves using HTML language to create hyperlinks.
     b.   is not possible yet, given current technology.
     c.   allows you to hear sounds over the Internet.
     d.   requires an expert to handle the programming.

d _____ 24.   Using white space in a document (p. 186)
     a.   is considered "cheating."
     b.   is only an option when you can't use color.
     c.   makes your document look unappealing.
     d.   provides contrast.

a _____ 25.   Justified type will (p. 187)
     a.   darken your message's appearance.
     b.   lighten your message's appearance.
     c.   distract from your message.
     d.   create more white space in your message.

c _____ 26.   Serif typefaces are preferable to sans serif faces for (p. 187)
     a.   display treatments.
     b.   headings and captions.
     c.   large blocks of text.
     d.   none of the above.

a _____ 27.   When selecting typefaces for a business document (pp. 187–188)
     a.   avoid using more than two typefaces on a page.
     b.   make generous use of such styles as all caps, underlines, and boldface.
     c.   choose a nice sans serif face for your main body text.
     d.   all of the above.

c _____ 28.   For effective document design (p. 188)
     a.   take readability formulas into account.
     b.   use as many decorative touches as possible, to make the pages look more interesting.
     c.   balance the space devoted to text, artwork, and white space.
     d.   all of the above.

d _____ 29. When you send the same document to a large number of people and you want each one to be personally addressed, you can use (p. 189)
   a. HTML.
   b. CD-ROMs.
   c. file merge software.
   d. mail merge software.

b _____ 30. Fax machines are indispensable for international businesses because they (p. 189)
   a. overcome the status problems that can exist between employees at various levels of the corporation.
   b. overcome time-zone problems of trying to contact someone by telephone.
   c. decrease the pressure to perform.
   d. decrease the flow of information around the world.

FILL-INS

1. In the first phase of editing, you should pay particular attention to the _____ and _____ of the message. (p. 164)

2. You use a _____ _____ to give you a rough idea of how educated your audience must be to read your message. (p. 167)

3. Word combinations that are needlessly repetitive are called _____ . (p. 170)

4. A _____ sentence is a series of two or more sentences unwisely connected by *and*. (p. 171)

5. With _____ construction, two are more similar ideas are expressed with the same grammatical pattern. (p. 172)

6. A modifier is said to be _____ when it has no real connection to the subject of the sentence. (p. 173)

7. _____ verbs are those that have been changed into nouns or adjectives. (p. 173)

8. The dominant tool for creating printed documents is _____ software. (p. 177)

9. A _____ is any standard block of text used in various documents without being changed. (p. 179)

10. A _____ is a device that takes a picture of a printed document and converts it to an electronic format. (p. 180)

11. Using a _____ is a wonderful way to weed out major typos, but you can't use it to replace good spelling skills. (p. 181)

12. A computer _____ gives you alternative words. (p. 182)

13. Use _____ _____ software to take advantage of specialized tools for formatting and designing your document. (pp. 184–185)

14. Space on a page that is free of text or artwork is called _____ space. (p. 186)

ANSWERS

1. beginning, ending
2. readability formula
3. redundancies
4. strung-on
5. parallel
6. dangling
7. camouflaged

8. word-processing
9. boilerplate
10. scanner
11. spell checker
12. thesaurus
13. desktop publishing
14. white

CHAPTER 7
WRITING ROUTINE, GOOD-NEWS, AND GOODWILL MESSAGES

TRUE OR FALSE

T _____ 1. Whenever you can assume that your audience will be interested in what you have to say or be willing to cooperate with you, use the direct approach. (p. 200)

F _____ 2. When making direct requests, you avoid such softening words and phrases as "please" and "I would appreciate." (p. 201)

T _____ 3. When making a direct request, you state what you want in the first sentence or two and then follow with an explanation. (p. 202)

F _____ 4. If the middle section of your request letter contains a series of questions, the most important question is saved for last. (p. 202)

T _____ 5. When writing a letter of request, avoid asking for information you can find on your own, even if it would take you considerable time. (p. 202)

T _____ 6. A letter of request closes with a request for a specific response, an expression of appreciation, and information on how the writer can be reached. (p. 203)

F _____ 7. In the final section of a request message, thank the reader in advance for cooperating. (p. 203)

F _____ 8. "I am pleased to inform you that . . ." is a good standard opening for a positive message. (p. 204)

F _____ 9. Because of the potential amount of detail required, an order is considered a particularly complex type of request. (p. 205)

F _____ 10. To avoid miscalculation, you always leave it up to the supplier to determine the amount you owe for an order. (p. 206)

F _____ 11. Because of their simple organization, routine requests require little tact. (p. 208)

F _____ 12. Writing routine requests is easy because tone and wording are not important in such messages. (p. 208)

F _____ 13. There is no reason to put requests to fellow employees in writing. (p. 208)

F _____ 14. Past customers are usually irritated if a company sends a letter of inquiry trying to reestablish the relationship. (p. 210)

T _____ 15. A computerized form letter prepared with care may be more personal and sincere than a quickly dictated "personal" reply to a request for information. (p. 211)

F _____ 16. Dissatistifed customers rarely tell others about their complaints. (p. 211)

T _____ 17. A written claim letter is preferable to a phone call or visit because it documents the customer's dissatisfaction. (p. 213)

T _____ 18. The person in an organization who receives and reads claim letters is rarely the one responsible for the problem. (pp. 213)

T _____ 19. When writing a claim letter, assume that a fair adjustment will be made. (p. 213)

F _____ 20. A claim letter or request for adjustment follows the indirect plan. (p. 213)

T _____ 21. When responding to claim letters, companies usually accept the customer's explanation of the problem. (p. 213)

T _____ 22. It's best to back up all claims and requests for adjustments with invoices, sales receipts, and so on; send copies to the company and keep the originals. (p. 213)

T _____ 23. An ungracious adjustment may increase customer dissatisfaction. (p. 215)

F _____ 24. When replying to a customer's complaint when your company is at fault, be sure to promise that the mistake will never happen again. (p. 215)

T _____ 25. A claim letter written as a personal answer to a unique situation starts with a clear statement of the good news. (p. 215)

F _____ 26. When you agree to make an adjustment even though the buyer technically was at fault, a courteous tone is less important. (p. 217)

F _____ 27. When a third party is at fault, the best approach is to refer the customer to that party to resolve the problem. (p. 217)

F _____ 28. A request for credit always takes the indirect approach. (p. 217)

T _____ 29. Letters approving credit are good-news letters. (p. 218)

F _____ 30. It's not necessary to ask someone's permission before listing his or her name as a job reference. (p. 220)

F _____ 31. Because recommendation letters are usually seen by the job candidate, the letter writer must be guarded in what he or she says. (p. 220)

T _____ 32. The most difficult recommendation letters to write are those for truly outstanding candidates. (p. 221)

F _____ 33. When writing a letter of recommendation, omit references to the candidate's shortcomings if they will keep him or her from getting the job. (p. 222)

T _____ 34. Because a letter telling someone that he or she got the job is a legal document, you need to make sure that all statements in the letter are accurate. (p. 224)

T _____ 35. News releases are typed on plain paper or on special letterhead, not on regular letterhead. (p. 225)

T _____ 36. Goodwill messages are friendly, unexpected notes with no direct business purpose. (p. 226)

T _____ 37. In a goodwill message, honesty and sincerity must come across above all else. (p. 227)

F _____ 38. You don't send notes of congratulation that deal with personal events unless you know the recipient well. (p. 228)

F _____ 39. When writing a letter of condolence, you should avoid making any offers of help. (p. 230)

T _____ 40. The goal when writing directives and instructions is to make the point so obvious and the steps so self-explanatory that the reader will not need to ask for additional help. (p. 230)

MULTIPLE CHOICE

c _____ 1. When making a direct request, you begin with (p. 200)
   a. an indication of the importance of your request.
   b. a statement of who you are.
   c. a clear statement of the main idea or request.
   d. a question.

b _____ 2. When making a request, you (p. 201)
   a. use the inductive plan.
   b. assume the reader will comply with your request.
   c. demand immediate action.
   d. do all of the above.

b _____ 3. In the middle section of a request message, you (p. 202)
   a. beg the reader to grant your request.
   b. give details of your request.
   c. give your sales pitch.
   d. do all of the above.

c _____ 4. When asking questions in a request message (p. 202)
   a. begin with the least important question and work your way up to the most important.
   b. avoid any open-ended questions.
   c. avoid asking for information that you can find on your own.
   d. do all of the above.

c _____ 5. When closing a direct request, you (p. 203)
a.   thank the reader in advance for helping you.
b.   mention your own qualifications or status.
c.   request a specific response and mention the time limits.
d.   indicate the consequences of a failure to reply.

c _____ 6. In a positive message, the main idea is presented (p. 203)
a.   in the first sentence of the middle paragraph.
b.   at the end of the middle paragraph.
c.   right at the beginning of the letter.
d.   in the last sentence of the letter.

d _____ 7. To achieve a clear, concise opening to a positive message, you (p. 203)
a.   make an outline.
b.   begin by stating your name, position, and why you are writing.
c.   concentrate on achieving goodwill.
d.   have a clear idea of the main point of the message.

c _____ 8. The middle section of a positive message (p. 204)
a.   establishes the tone.
b.   states the main idea.
c.   is the longest part.
d.   does all of the above.

a _____ 9. A good beginning for an order letter would be (pp. 205–206)
a.   Please send the following items.
b.   Hi! My name is Louise Sjoberg and I'd like to place an order.
c.   Enclosed is a check for $62.40.
d.   Do you offer discounts for quantity purchases?

c _____ 10. Routine requests (p. 208)
a.   need not be tactful if they are brief.
b.   follow the inductive format.
c.   may go to hundreds or even thousands of people and thus have major potential for creating a good impression or causing ill will.
d.   are always made orally.

a _____ 11. Individuals outside an organization might respond more readily to a request if they are told (p. 210)
a.   how the request benefits them.
b.   how many others have replied favorably.
c.   how easy it will be to say yes.
d.   why they have been selected.

a _____ 12. A human resources department that receives a lot of inquiries about job openings would best deal with this repetitive task by (p. 211)
a.   using a carefully crafted computerized form letter.
b.   answering each one personally.
c.   not responding if there are no job openings.
d.   making most responses by phone.

d _____ 13. When a potential sale is involved, after you present the key information, you should (p. 211)
    a. promptly and courteously end the letter.
    b. provide a clear, conversational statement of the main point.
    c. urge the customer to reply immediately.
    d. include resale and sales promotion information.

c _____ 14. When writing a claim letter, the best way to begin is by (p. 213)
    a. complimenting the company for past service.
    b. providing a detailed description of the faulty merchandise.
    c. stating the problem clearly and specifically.
    d. threatening legal action if you do not receive a favorable adjustment.

a _____ 15. When responding to a customer request for an adjustment, it is usually sensible to assume that (p. 213)
    a. the customer's account of the situation is truthful.
    b. the customer's account of the situation is exaggerated.
    c. the customer is hostile.
    d. the customer is trying to pull a fast one.

d _____ 16. When responding to a customer complaint about one of your company's services, you (p. 215)
    a. soften the situation with excuses such as "Nobody's perfect" or "Mistakes will happen."
    b. use a generous, grudging tone.
    c. use a standard form letter, with blanks left for filling in unique information in neat handwriting.
    d. avoid blaming a specific individual or department for the problem.

c _____ 17. Companies that receive large numbers of customer claims per year often develop (p. 215)
    a. crippling legal and financial problems.
    b. a policy of nonresponse to all customer inquiries.
    c. customized form letters to speed the response to customers' claims.
    d. none of the above.

b _____ 18. The opening of a letter responding to a request for adjustment (p. 215)
    a. starts with flattery to soften the customer up.
    b. is "you" oriented.
    c. apologizes for the problem.
    d. promises that the problem will never happen again.

d _____ 19. If a customer requesting an adjustment is at fault for the problem, the best response is to (pp. 216–217)
    a. refuse the claim without any explanation.
    b. refuse the claim and point out the customer's mistake.
    c. honor the claim but do so begrugdlingly.
    d. honor the claim but tactfully point out that your firm was not at fault.

b _____ 20.   When responding to a request for adjustment when a third party is at fault, the best approach is to (p. 217)
   a.   refuse the claim and suggest that the customer sue the third party.
   b.   refuse the claim but forward the paperwork to the third party.
   c.   honor the claim with no additional explanation.
   d.   honor the claim but explain that your company was not at fault.

c _____ 21.   The closing section of a letter approving a credit application (p. 219)
   a.   states the upper limit of the account.
   b.   indicates due dates for payments and interest charges for unpaid balances.
   c.   provides resale information and sales promotion.
   d.   states credit terms in an authoritarian tone.

c _____ 22.   Before volunteering someone's name as a reference, always (p. 220)
   a.   assume you have permission to do so.
   b.   describe your relationship with that person.
   c.   ask that person's permission.
   d.   list that person's address and phone number for ease of contact.

a _____ 23.   If you request a recommendation from a person you haven't had contact with recently, you should (p. 220)
   a.   use the opening of your letter to refresh the person's memory.
   b.   enclose a stamped, preaddressed envelope.
   c.   use the persuasive approach.
   d.   use the bad-news approach.

a _____ 24.   When writing a letter of recommendation, you (pp. 221–222)
   a.   should use careful wording that will meet both parties' needs.
   b.   show it to the job candidate before sending it to the person who requested it.
   c.   overstate the candidate's abilities if he or she is a good friend and really wants the job.
   d.   make sure to include any negative stories you've heard about the candidate.

b _____ 25.   It may be unethical to omit negative information from a recommendation if (p. 222)
   a.   the information is well-known in the workplace.
   b.   the information is true and relevant.
   c.   the applicant asks you to do so.
   d.   the position is a high-ranking one.

c _____ 26.   If you have negative comments to express regarding the qualifications of a job candidate, it's best to (p. 222)
   a.   keep them to yourself.
   b.   include others' criticisms to support your statements.
   c.   place your criticism in the context of a generally favorable recommendation.
   d.   state your opinion strongly, since it is protected by the First Amendment.

c _____ 27.   News releases are (pp. 225–226)
   a.   typed on regular company letterhead.
   b.   single spaced.
   c.   written to match the style of the medium they are intended for.
   d.   all of the above.

c _____ 28.   The purpose of goodwill messages is to (p. 226)
     a.   make a sales pitch.
     b.   convey good news about products and operations.
     c.   enhance relationships with customers and other businesspeople.
     d.   offer help to those in need.

c _____ 29.   Condolence messages (pp. 229–230)
     a.   should never offer assistance to the recipient.
     b.   should make as little reference to the deceased as possible.
     c.   should avoid flowery writing and euphemisms like "passing away."
     d.   all of the above.

a _____ 30.   Directives and instructions are considered routine messages because (p. 230)
     a.   readers are assumed to be willing to comply.
     b.   they are so frequently written.
     c.   they do not require specific action.
     d.   they contain good news.

FILL-INS

1.   The _____ of a routine request states what you want. (p. 202)

2.   The _____ of a routine request provides justification, explanation, and details. (p. 202)

3.   The _____ of a direct request makes a request for a specific response and expresses appreciation or goodwill. (p. 203)

4.   A _____ request for information is simple and straightforward. (p. 208)

5.   Because many requests are similar, companies usually develop _____ letters to respond to these repetitive queries. (p. 211)

6.   Dissatisfied customers explain their problems in _____ letters. (p. 211)

7.   Before volunteering someone's name as a _____, ask that person's permission. (p. 220)

8.   In most cases, a letter of _____ is a confidential discussion of a job applicant's qualifications. (p. 220)

9. Making a false and malicious written statement about someone constitutes _____. (p. 222)

10. _____ _____ are documents that convey company news to the media. (p. 225)

11. Friendly notes with no direct business purpose, such as those conveying congratulations or thanks, are called _____ messages. (p. 226)

12. Messages of _____ recognize the contributions of employees or business associates. (p. 229)

13. _____ are memos that tell employees what to do. (p. 230)

14. _____ tell readers how to do something. (p. 230)

ANSWERS

1. beginning (opening)
2. middle
3. closing (ending)
4. routine
5. form
6. claim (adjustment)
7. reference

8. recommendation
9. libel
10. news releases
11. goodwill
12. appreciation
13. directives
14. instructions

CHAPTER 8
WRITING BAD-NEWS MESSAGES

TRUE OR FALSE

T _____ 1.   When presenting bad news you need to help the reader understand that your unfavorable decision is based on a business judgment, not a personal one. (p. 246)

T _____ 2.   You can help establish the right tone in a bad-news message by making liberal use of the "you" attitude. (p. 247)

T _____ 3.   Words that should not appear in a bad-news letter include *unfortunately, regret,* and *inconvenience,* because they're negative and counterproductive. (p. 247)

T _____ 4.   Sometimes the "you" attitude is best observed by avoiding the word *you.* (p. 247)

T _____ 5.   When using the indirect plan for a bad-news message, you present the reasons for your decision before revealing the bad news itself. (p. 248)

F _____ 6.   You use a buffer to make the reader think that good news will follow. (pp. 248–249)

F _____ 7.   You can start off the buffer to a bad-news message with the bad news itself as long as you state it reasonably. (pp. 248–249)

T _____ 8.   It's best to avoid using a know-it-all tone in a bad-news message. (p. 249)

F _____ 9.   A good buffer begins with an apology. (p. 249)

T _____ 10. When presenting bad news, it is important to say *why* you have reached the decision before you say *what* the decision is. (p. 250)

T _____ 11. Even when you are presenting bad news, you try to explain how your decision will ultimately benefit the reader. (p. 250)

F _____ 12. It is a good idea to use "company policy" as a cushion when presenting reasons for bad news. (p. 250)

F _____ 13. When turning down someone for a job, it is best to come right out and say, "You do not meet our requirements." (p. 251)

T _____ 14. You do not go into the specific reasons for bad news if those reasons are confidential, excessively complicated, or purely negative. (p. 251)

T _____ 15. You can de-emphasize bad news by minimizing the space or time devoted to it. (p. 251)

F _____ 16.   In a bad-news message, you never give the reader any indication that he or she could have received or might someday receive a favorable answer. (p. 251)

T _____ 17.   Statements beginning "I must refuse" and "We cannot allow" are particularly likely to offend readers. (p. 252)

T _____ 18.   It's best to end a bad-news message on a positive note. (p. 252)

F _____ 19.   In the close to a bad-news message, you repeat the bad news. (p. 252)

F _____ 20.   The close of a bad-news message should urge additional communication from the reader. (p. 252)

F _____ 21.   The direct plan is never used for bad-news messages. (p. 252)

T _____ 22.   A bad-news message organized according to the direct plan has no buffer. (p. 253)

T _____ 23.   An advantage of the direct plan for communicating bad news is that it keeps the message short. (p. 253)

T _____ 24.   You would use the direct plan for bad-news messages when the message has little or no personal impact on the audience. (p. 253)

T _____ 25.   If you were writing a memo to inform your company's bookkeeping department about price hikes in your products, you would use the direct plan. (p. 255)

F _____ 26.   Always use the direct plan when denying a request for information. (p. 256)

F _____ 27.   When you need to inform customers that part of their order must be back-ordered, the direct plan is preferable because part of your message is good news. (p. 257)

T _____ 28.   When you must back-order for a customer, a strong close encourages a favorable attitude toward the entire transaction. (p. 257)

F _____ 29.   When refusing adjustments of claims, use the direct plan in most cases. (p. 259)

T _____ 30.   When refusing to make an adjustment, avoid calling the customer defamatory names, such as *cheat* or *liar*. (p. 260)

F _____ 31.   Written defamation is called slander. (p. 260)

T _____ 32.   A letter denying credit to a business is more factual and less personal than a letter denying credit to an individual. (p. 262)

F _____ 33.   To avoid trouble, you handle credit denials over the phone, instead of in writing. (p. 262)

T _____ 34.   Some employers refuse to write recommendation letters. (p. 264)

T _____ 35.   In a letter turning down a job applicant, you should open with the direct plan. (p. 265)

F _____ 36. Employee performance reviews are inadmissible as evidence in any lawsuits against an employer. (p. 267)

F _____ 37. The best method for delivering performance reviews is by e-mail or fax. (p. 268)

T _____ 38. A termination letter should present specific reasons for why the employee is being asked to leave. (p. 270)

T _____ 39. In messages delivering bad news about company operations or performance, the focus should be on the reasons for the bad news. (p. 271)

F _____ 40. It's better for customers and shareholders to hear about a company's performance problems from newspapers than from the company itself . (p. 271)

MULTIPLE CHOICE

b _____ 1. When composing a bad-news message, you (p. 246)
   a. choose a buffer that will distract your reader from the main point of your message.
   c. try to gain the audience's acceptance of the bad news.
   c. leave the reader with hope that you will change your decision.
   d. do all of the above.

a _____ 2. Avoid words such as *regret, error, fault,* and *unfortunately* because (p. 247)
   a. they create a negative tone and are counterproductive.
   b. they are too abstract.
   c. they imply that you are apologizing.
   d. they are impersonal and passive.

c _____ 3. Which of the following would be an inappropriate use of the word "you" in a bad-news letter? (p. 247)
   a. "You possess many fine skills."
   b. "The frying pan you ordered is being shipped today."
   c. "You shouldn't have washed that wool shirt; it should be dry cleaned only."
   d. "When you have more managerial experience, we encourage you to reapply."

b _____ 4. Instead of beginning your message with a blunt no, you can use (p. 248)
   a. the direct plan.
   b. the indirect plan.
   c. a combination of the direct and indirect plans.
   d. the deductive plan.

c _____ 5. Following the indirect plan, the bad news comes (p. 248)
   a. immediately after the buffer.
   b. immediately before the reasons.
   c. immediately after the reasons.
   d. at the very end.

c _____ 6.   The point of using the indirect plan is to (p. 248)
    a.   keep readers in the dark about the bad news.
    b.   keep your company's best interests foremost.
    c.   ease your audience into the part of your message that shows you are fair-minded.
    d.   save face for your company.

a _____ 7.   A neutral lead-in to bad news is called (p. 248)
    a.   a buffer.
    b.   a disclaimer.
    c.   an apology.
    d.   a refusal.

c _____ 8.   If possible, base the buffer for your bad-news message on (p. 249)
    a.   company policy.
    b.   an interesting bit of news.
    c.   statements made by the person you're responding to.
    d.   the weather.

d _____ 9.   Building up the reader at the beginning of your bad-news message will (p. 249)
    a.   make the bad news easier to take.
    b.   make you look better later.
    c.   keep the letter positive.
    d.   make the reader's subsequent letdown even more painful.

d _____10.   The buffer of a bad-news message (p. 249)
    a.   avoids saying no.
    b.   avoids wordy phrases.
    c.   avoids apologizing.
    d.   avoids all of the above.

c _____ 11.   A good opening for a bad-news message would be (p. 249)
    a.   "I'm sorry to say I have some bad news."
    b.   "This letter is in reply to your application."
    c.   "Your résumé shows an admirable breadth of experience."
    d.   "We have no openings at this time."

b _____ 12.   In a bad-news message, the reasons for the decision (p. 249)
    a.   are so obvious that you don't need to mention them.
    b.   come directly after the buffer and follow naturally from it.
    c.   are glossed over quickly.
    d.   are long and roundabout to cushion the negative aspects.

a _____ 13.   In the reasons section of a bad-news message, you (p. 250)
    a.   present enough detail for the audience to understand your reasons.
    b.   explain what your decision is before you explain why you have reached it.
    c.   apologize for the negative decision.
    d.   do all of the above.

d _____ 14. A good way to make bad news less painful is to (p. 251)
- a. maximize the space devoted to it.
- b. say, "I trust our decision is satisfactory."
- c. avoid stating it and hope that the reader understands what you mean.
- d. de-emphasize it by burying it in the middle of a sentence or paragraph.

a _____ 15. When rejecting a job applicant, you can soften the blow by (p. 251)
- a. focusing on the positive and only implying the bad news.
- b. mentioning the qualifications of the person who was hired.
- c. telling the applicant how many others he or she was competing against.
- d. apologizing for wasting the person's time.

c _____ 16. When delivering bad news, wording such as "We must turn down," "Much as I would like to," and "We cannot afford to" (p. 252)
- a. softens the blow by drawing attention away from reader and onto the sender.
- b. will impress the reader as being straightforward and forceful.
- c. is likely to cause pain and anger in the reader.
- d. is unavoidable.

b _____ 17. In the closing of a bad-news message, you (p. 252)
- a. encourage the person to write or call to discuss the situation further.
- b. build goodwill by ending on a positive note.
- c. ask for feedback on whether the decision is acceptable to the reader.
- d. express concern over possibly losing the reader's business.

c _____ 18. When you use the direct plan for a bad-news message, you (p. 252)
- a. still need to include a buffer.
- b. have more room to discuss pertinent details.
- c. can get right to the point.
- d. can expect your audience to be offended.

b _____ 19. Use the direct plan with a bad-news message if (p. 253)
- a. the message will have a great deal of personal impact on members of the audience.
- b. you want to present an image of firmness and strength.
- c. an order is unfillable or portions of it must be back-ordered.
- d. you are refusing to make an adjustment on a claim.

c _____ 20. When you are refusing an invitation or a request, you (p. 257)
- a. always use the indirect approach.
- b. always use the direct approach.
- c. consider your relationship with the reader.
- d. use the direct approach when your denial is likely to disappoint the reader.

c _____ 21. When you must notify a customer that you can send only part of an order, the buffer (p. 257)
- a. gives the reason for the delay on the balance of the order.
- b. states the approximate length of time the customer will have to wait for a decision.
- c. emphasizes the good news that part of the order is on its way.
- d. does all of the above.

b _____ 22. A woman returns a formal dress to your store. It is soiled and has a rip at the hem line, but she says she is returning it unworn because it doesn't fit. How do you inform her of your refusal to give her a refund? (p. 260)
- a. State that company policy prevents you from accepting the return but that if you had anything to say about it you'd take it back, no questions asked.
- b. Restate her complaint to let her know you understand it, explain as positively as possible that you are unable to accept the return of damaged merchandise, and recommend a seamstress who can fix the tear and alter the dress for her.
- c. Challenge the woman to try on the dress and prove that it doesn't fit.
- d. Use humor to soften the blow of your refusal.

c _____ 23. To avoid being accused of defamation when you refuse an adjustment (p. 260)
- a. make all refusals by phone instead of in writing.
- b. explain why you are making the refusal.
- c. consult your company's legal department or an attorney if you think a message might have legal consequences.
- d. all of the above.

a _____ 24. If you defame someone in a letter (p. 260)
- a. it is considered libel.
- b. it is considered slander
- c. you don't need to be able to prove that your accusations are true.
- d. all of the above.

b _____ 25. When giving your reasons for denying a credit request, you point out (p. 262)
- a. that your company can't afford to take on bad risks.
- b. how your decision will help the customer keep from becoming overextended.
- c. that company policy has dictated the decision.
- d. that it's not your fault that the credit was denied.

a _____ 26. Denials of business credit, as opposed to denials of individual credit, are (p. 262)
- a. less personally sensitive but more financially significant.
- b. less financially significant but more personally sensitive.
- c. more routine and require less detail.
- d. legally binding and require a lawyer's approval.

c _____ 27. A letter to a prospective employer refusing to provide a recommendation (p. 264)
- a. is considered unethical; these requests should not be refused.
- b. should follow the indirect plan.
- c. should be brief and factual.
- d. all of the above.

a _____ 28. A letter rejecting a job applicant should (p. 265)
- a. open with the direct plan.
- b. point out the applicant's shortcomings.
- c. be as personal as possible.
- d. be as long as possible.

b _____ 29.   If you must give an employee a negative performance review (pp. 267–268)
         a.   do so by e-mail or fax.
         b.   confront the problem right away.
         c.   limit your discussion to the areas where the employee needs improvement.
         d.   all of the above.

b _____ 30.   When you need to inform stakeholders that your company is having serious problems (p. 271)
         a.   the best approach is to leak the news to the press rather than make a public announcement.
         b.   minimize the bad news by presenting it in as favorable a light as possible.
         c.   use the direct approach.
         d.   use as many hedging words as possible.

FILL-INS

1.   Denying requests, refusing adjustments on claims, and refusing to extend credit are all types of _____ messages. (p. 247)

2.   When composing bad-news messages, it is important to establish an appropriate _____. (p. 247)

3.   You can ease the pain of a bad-news message by using _____ words. (p. 247)

4.   In the _____ plan for bad-news messages, the negative decision comes after the reasons supporting the decision. (p. 248)

5.   Using the indirect plan, you begin your message with a _____ that softens the blow of the bad news. (p. 248)

6.   Your reasons for a negative decision should convince your audience that the decision is justified, _____, and logical. (p. 250)

7.   A message organized on the _____ plan starts with a clear statement of the bad news. (p. 252)

8.   When turning down an _____ or a request for a favor, use the direct plan if you know the person well. (p. 257)

9.   When an item is temporarily out of stock and you must back-order it for a customer, you use the _____ plan. (p. 257)

10. A false statement that tends to damage someone's character or reputation is called _____. (p. 260)

11. Written defamation is called _____. (p. 260)

12. Spoken defamation is called _____. (p. 260)

13. A _____ review is a manager's formal or informal evaluation of an employee. (p. 266)

14. When writing a _____ letter, present specific justifications for asking the employee to leave. (p. 270)

ANSWERS

1. bad-news
2. tone
3. positive
4. indirect
5. buffer
6. fair
7. direct

8. invitation
9. indirect
10. defamation
11. libel
12. slander
13. performance
14. termination

CHAPTER 9
WRITING PERSUASIVE MESSAGES

TRUE OR FALSE

F _____ 1.   Persuasion can be defined as asking somebody to do something. (p. 288)

F _____ 2.   Even though people may have different needs, they will respond to a given message in much the same way. (p. 288)

T _____ 3.   To devise an effective persuasive message, you need to analyze audience members and then appeal to their needs. (p. 288)

F _____ 4.   Demographics refers to the pyshological characteristics of an individual, such as personality, attitudes, and lifestyle. (p. 289)

T _____ 5.   One of the best ways to gain credibility for your message is to support it with objective evidence. (p. 292)

F _____ 6.   The term AIDA refers to a computer program used to compose persuasive messages. (p 293)

T _____ 7.   In the attention phase of a persuasive letter, you tell the audience what is in the message for them. (p. 293)

T _____ 8.   The interest section of a persuasive letter provides details on how the message is related to the audience. (p. 293)

T _____ 9.   The purpose of the desire section of a persuasive letter is to convince readers that they really need to take the action that the message urges. (p. 293)

T _____ 10. All persuasive messages end with a section that urges specific action. (p. 293)

F _____ 11. When writing persuasive messages, you are careful not to mix emotional and logical appeals. (p. 295)

T _____ 12. Abstract concepts such as *freedom, prestige,* or *success* can be used to enhance the emotional content of persuasive messages. (p. 295)

F _____ 13. Induction refers to reasoning from a generalization to a specific conclusion. (p. 296)

T _____ 14. An argument or statement can appear to be true when it is really false. (p. 296)

T _____ 15. In the Toulmin logic model, you support your claim with evidence that is itself backed by a chain of reasons. (p. 296)

T _____ 16.   An example of faulty logic is to assume that one event caused another just because it happened first. (p. 296)

T _____ 17.   Semantics is a tool you can use to strengthen your persuasive message. (p. 297)

F _____ 18.   In developing persuasive messages, you should avoid the use of metaphors, as they will only confuse the reader. (p. 299)

T _____ 19.   If you expect a hostile audience, you should be careful to present all sides of an issue before making the case for your own argument. (p. 299)

F _____ 20.   When making a persuasive request, you can offer no benefits to the reader and thus must appeal to his or her altruistic tendencies. (p. 300)

F _____ 21.   When writing a persuasive claim or request for adjustment, you are basically just getting the complaint off your chest. (p. 301)

T _____ 22.   When writing a persuasive claim or request for adjustment, you should focus on the benefits of solving the problem rather than the horrors of neglecting your complaint. (p. 303)

T _____ 23.   The purpose of a sales letter is to motivate people to spend money on products. (p. 305)

F _____ 24.   It is perfectly legal to use someone's name or photograph in a sales letter without the person's permission as long as he or she is a public figure. (p. 346)

T _____ 25.   The main idea in a sales letter revolves around a selling point and related consumer benefits. (p. 306)

T _____ 26.   Sales letters are prepared according to the AIDA plan. (p. 309)

F _____ 27.   For opening sales letters, all attention-getting devices are equally effective. (p. 309)

F _____ 28.   When writing a sales letter, you narrow your focus to five main selling points. (p. 310)

T _____ 29.   If low price is a major benefit of your product, you can display it prominently in your sales letter. (p. 311)

T _____ 30.   When writing a sales letter, your overriding purpose is to persuade readers to take immediate action. (p. 312)

F _____ 31.   Most of the techniques used in writing sales letters are inappropriate for fund-raising messages. (p. 312)

T _____ 32.   When you write a fund-raising letter, be sure that the benefits you emphasize relate to what your donors want, not what your organization does. (p. 313)

T _____ 33.   Fund-raising letters depend heavily on emotional appeals. (p. 313)

T _____ 34.   The purpose of the collection process is to maintain goodwill while collecting what is owed. (p. 315)

F _____ 35.   A good and perfectly legal way to shame someone into paying a debt is to tell the person's employer or relatives about the debt. (p. 315)

F _____ 36.   Laws protecting debtors prevent you from getting tough in collection letters, such as giving the debtor an ultimatum. (p. 318)

F _____ 37.   In collection letters, negative appeals are usually more effective than positive ones. (p. 318)

T _____ 38.   The typical collection series consists of a notification, a reminder, an inquiry, an urgent notice, and an ultimatum. (p. 318)

F _____ 39.   If a debtor does not respond to a reminder letter within 10 days, your next step is to sue for the money owed. (p. 319)

T _____ 40.   The tone of an ultimatum doesn't need to be as personal and helpful as early notes in the collection series. (p. 320)

MULTIPLE CHOICE

b _____ 1.   The process of influencing people's attitudes or actions is called (p. 288)
   a.   strategic planning.
   b.   persuasion.
   c.   coercion.
   d.   nonverbal communication.

c _____ 2.   Which of the following is *not* an example of demographic information? (p. 289)
   a.   age.
   b.   occupation.
   c.   lifestyle.
   d.   income.

b _____ 3.   Personality, lifestyle, and attitudes are assessed through (p. 289)
   a.   demographic surveys.
   b.   psychographic studies.
   c.   inkblot tests.
   d.   examining census data.

c _____ 4.   To build credibility with your audience, you (p. 292)
   a.   come right out and state that you are trustworthy.
   b.   let them know that you're not rigid about what you have to say.
   c.   are enthusiastic about the subject of your message.
   d.   point out ways in which your knowledge is superior to that of your audience members.

d _____ 5.   AIDA stands for (p. 293)
     a.   appeal, indirect, direct, action.
     b.   anticipate inquiry in doing adjustments.
     c.   assume, insist, describe, act.
     d.   attention, interest, desire, action.

b _____ 6.   The purpose of the interest section of a persuasive message is to (p. 293)
     a.   capture attention.
     b.   stress how the information in the message will benefit the audience.
     c.   increase the audience's desire to take the action that is recommended in the message.
     d.   get the reader to act immediately.

c _____ 7.   The purpose of the desire section of a persuasive message is to (p. 293)
     a.   introduce the main idea.
     b.   create interest in the main idea.
     c.   increase your audience's willingness to take action.
     d.   suggest the action your audience should take.

a _____ 8.   An effective ending for a persuasive message would be (p. 293)
     a.   "Return the enclosed coupon by June 15 and you'll receive your bonus 'early bird' key chain."
     b.   "Please respond as soon as possible."
     c.   "Wouldn't you like to save some money?"
     d.   "Be sure to tell all your friends about this exciting offer."

d _____ 9.   When writing persuasive messages, one way to avoid faulty logic is to (p. 296)
     a.   avoid induction.
     b.   avoid deduction.
     c.   avoid praising your opponent.
     d.   avoid hasty generalizations.

d _____ 10.   An ethical persuasive argument is supported by (p. 296)
     a.   a restatement of the claim in different words.
     b.   information about the opponent's character.
     c.   any evidence you can come up with, whether or not it's relevant.
     d.   points or principles that can be proven or that your audience already accepts or agrees on.

b _____ 11.   To overcome audience resistance to your message (p. 299)
     a.   use the hard-sell approach.
     b.   present all sides of the issue before making the case for your position.
     c.   resist compromise.
     d.   do all of the above.

b _____ 12.   When writing a persuasive request for action, you (p. 301)
     a.   use the direct approach.
     b.   demonstrate that helping you will indeed solve a significant problem.
     c.   ask for more than you actually want so that you'll have a cushion for negotiation.
     d.   avoid flattery.

a _____ 13. The most important thing to remember when preparing a persuasive request for information is to (p. 301)
   a. keep your request from being too general or all-encompassing.
   b. ask the reader to provide as much information as possible.
   c. ask your reader to save you time and effort by supplying the information.
   d. make yourself look good in the reader's eyes.

c _____ 14. Which of the following would be considered a selling point of a car phone? (p. 307)
   a. status
   b. safety
   c. portability
   d. none of the above

b _____ 15. As you consider the benefits of your product, in your sales letter you will ultimately want to (p. 307)
   a. pick out three or four to call attention to.
   b. single out one benefit that will become the hallmark of your campaign.
   c. mention as many benefits as possible.
   d. choose one direct benefit and one indirect benefit.

b _____ 16. Which of the following is not one of the tried and true attention-getting devices used in sales letters? (p. 309)
   a. offering a free sample of the product
   b. insulting the reader
   c. a provocative question
   d. a solution to a problem

b _____ 17. Asking "What does the competition offer?" "What is special about my product?" and "What are potential buyers really looking for?" helps you determine (p. 310)
   a. which tried-and-true attention-getter to use.
   b. your product's central selling point.
   c. the price for your product.
   d. which type of mailing list to use.

a _____ 18. If the audience for your sales letter promoting a new security system is made up of affluent suburbanites, the consumer benefit you would most want to emphasize in your letter is (p. 310)
   a. the reliability of the system when protecting the consumer's property.
   b. the low cost.
   c. the attractive appearance of the device.
   d. easy, do-it-yourself installation.

c _____ 19. Which of the following would be the best wording in a sales letter? (p. 311)
   a. "The NuForm desk chair is so comfortable that you won't want to go home from work."
   b. "The NuForm desk chair is designed to give your lower back the ultimate in support and to relieve pressure on your legs as well."
   c. "The NuForm desk chair supports your lower back and relieves pressure on your legs."
   d. "The incredibly handsome NuForm desk chair is functional as well as impressive; it provides a great deal of lower back support."

d _____ 20.   If price is one of your strong selling points, you (p. 311)
   a.   mention special offers, such as volume discounts, before actually stating the price.
   b.   compare the price to the cost of some other product or activity ("This exercise equipment costs less than a health club membership").
   c.   break the total price into smaller units ("Just six easy payments of $19.95 each will bring you this lovely collector's item").
   d.   emphasize it in the opening of the sales letter.

d _____ 21.   In a sales letter, product claims are (p. 311)
   a.   supported primarily by testimonials from satisfied customers.
   b.   supported primarily by statistics from scientific studies of the product.
   c.   supported primarily by background information on the company selling the product.
   d.   supported by as much information as possible, of many different types.

a _____ 22.   Before you start writing a fund-raising message, it is important for you to know (p. 313)
   a.   what donors want.
   b.   the dollar amount of your goal.
   c.   how wealthy the potential donors are.
   d.   all of the above.

b _____ 23.   In a fund-raising letter, you should (p. 313)
   a.   use the hard-sell approach.
   b.   keep your message as personal as possible.
   c.   make the message as long as possible.
   d.   emphasize the goals of your organization.

c _____ 24.   One common mistake in writing fund-raising messages is to (p. 313)
   a.   use slice-of-life stories.
   b.   make the message personal.
   c.   waste space on long warm-ups.
   d.   waste space writing about the reader instead of about the organization.

b _____ 25.   Which of the following is *not* a guideline for writing effective fund-raising messages? (p. 313)
   a.   use simple, warm, and personal language.
   b.   make the need clear but not so urgent that it is hard to say no.
   c.   explain why the money is needed.
   d.   make the need easy to respond to.

b _____ 26.   Conscientious customers who have not paid their bills (p. 318)
   a.   are simply irresponsible when it comes to money, so they need to be treated firmly.
   b.   are embarrassed about past-due accounts.
   c.   are deadbeats and will do anything to avoid paying.
   d.   are dissatisfied with their purchase and have refused to pay as a matter of principle.

a _____ 27. When preparing collection letters, you emphasize (p. 318)
   a. the benefits of complying with your request for payment.
   b. your power to force the customer to comply.
   c. that the person's friends and relatives will be asked to help pay the debt if payment is not forthcoming.
   d. all of the above.

c _____ 28. The typical collection series begins with (p. 318)
   a. an inquiry.
   b. a reminder.
   c. a notification.
   d. an urgent notice.

b _____ 29. If a customer has not responded to your notification of a payment due, the next step is to send (p. 318)
   a. an urgent notice.
   b. a reminder.
   c. an inquiry.
   d. an ultimatum.

d _____ 30. In an ultimatum to a debtor (p. 320)
   a. you can drop the kid gloves and become abusive.
   b. you can threaten a lawsuit, even if you don't intend to sue.
   c. you encourage the debtor to explain why it is taking him or her so long to respond to your collection letters.
   d. you state the exact consequences of nonpayment.

FILL-INS

1. _____ is the process of changing people's attitudes or influencing their actions. (p. 288)

2. People's _____ _____ needs must be met before they will seek to fulfill higher-level needs. (p. 289)

3. It is particularly important to establish _____ with a skeptical or hostile audience. (p. 292)

4. Persuasive messages often follow a specialized form of the indirect approach called the _____ plan. (p. 293)

5. _____ is reasoning from specific evidence to a general conclusion. (p. 296)

6. _____ is reasoning from a generalization to a specific conclusion. (p. 296)

7. _____ refers to the meaning of words and other symbols. (p. 297)

8. The purpose of _____ letters is to motivate people to spend money on products. (p. 305)

9. _____ _____ are the most attractive features of a product. (p. 306)

10. _____ are the particular advantages that readers will realize from the features of a product or idea. (p. 306)

11. A sales letter begins with some sort of _____ device. (p. 309)

12. The _____ _____ _____ is the single point around which you build your sales message. (p. 310)

13. The purpose of the _____ process is to maintain goodwill while recovering money that is owed. (p. 315)

14. The first message in the collection series is the letter of _____. (p. 318)

ANSWERS

1. persuasion
2. basic needs (lower-level needs)
3. credibility
4. AIDA
5. induction
6. deduction
7. semantics

8. sales
9. selling points
10. benefits
11. attention-getting
12. central selling point
13. collection
14. notification

CHAPTER 10
COMMUNICATING INFORMATION THROUGH THE INTERNET
AND OTHER TECHNOLOGIES

TRUE OR FALSE

T _____ 1. With today's technology, it's possible for people to run their entire business from their car. (p. 338)

T _____ 2. A disadvantage of new communications technology is that it has blurred the line between work life and home life. (p. 338)

F _____ 3. A "cookie" is a virus that is carried by the Internet and can infect a computer's hard drive. (p. 339)

T _____ 4. The Internet is the world's largest network of electronically connected computers. (p. 339)

F _____ 5. The Internet is owned by the U.S. government. (p. 339)

F _____ 6. The World Wide Web is a global interconnection of computers that is separate from the Internet. (p. 339)

T _____ 7. HTTP stands for "hypertext transfer protocol." (p. 339)

F _____ 8. In an URL, the ".com" suffix stands for "communication." (p. 340)

T _____ 9. It is now possible for Internet users to converse vocally over the Internet, without using a traditional phone. (p. 340)

F _____ 10. It takes most e-mail messages about a day to reach their destination, especially if it's thousands of miles away. (p. 341)

F _____ 11. A drawback of e-mail is that lower-level employees can easily send messages to top management. (p. 341)

T _____ 12. E-mail encourages greater collaboration among employees. (p. 341)

F _____ 13. People don't make as much use of e-mail as they could and should. (p. 342)

F _____ 14. Companies that have used videoconferencing are abandoning it because of the rising costs and inadequate quality associated with the equipment needed. (p. 342)

F _____ 15. FTP—"For The Parents"—is software designed for parents to use in preventing their kids from accessing particular Web sites. (p. 343)

T _____ 16.   A newsgroup is a place you visit to read posted messages, while a discussion mailing list actually delivers the messages directly to you. (p. 344)

F _____ 17.   A search engine and a directory are the same thing. (p. 344)

T _____ 18.   Each search engine has qualities that distinguish it from the others. (p. 345)

T _____ 19.   Portals, such as Microsoft Service Network, are Internet gateways. (p. 347)

F _____ 20.   Using a search engine to find information is an example of push technology. (p. 347)

F _____ 21.   Personal agents are services that you need to subscribe to at a hefty fee, but they're worth it because they deliver just the information you want from the Internet. (p. 348)

T _____ 22.   An intranet is a private corporate network that connects company computers in various locations. (p. 348)

T _____ 23.   A firewall is a special kind of gateway that controls access to an intranet. (p. 348)

T _____ 24.   One of the biggest advantages of an intranet is that it allows all the employees in a company to access it even if they are using different computer operating systems. (p. 349)

F _____ 25.   An exciting aspect of intranets is that they will automatically organize all the information for a company. (p. 351)

F _____ 26.   Once a company installs an intranet, employees generally abandon their familiar systems and flock to it. (p. 352)

T _____ 27.   An extranet allows prequalified outsiders to have access to a company's intranet. (p. 352)

F _____ 28.   Extranets are good for public relations, but they tend to be costly in the long run. (p. 352)

T _____ 29.   Many business users of new technology have abandoned politeness and manners in their electronic communications. (p. 351)

T _____ 30.   A call-management system is a type of business phone system that gives companies better control over the calls that come in and go out. (p. 353)

F _____ 31.   Because of government regulations and technological requirements, the cost of wireless phones is expected to go up over the next several years. (p. 354)

T _____ 32.   New technology now allows several voices, faxes, and e-mail messages to all travel over the same phone line at the same time. (p. 354)

F _____ 33.   Voice-mail systems are basically glorified answering machines. (p. 354)

F _____ 34.   The accuracy of speech-recognition systems is only slightly reduced if multiple people are talking or if the speaker has a foreign accent. (p. 356)

T _____ 35. People are finding it more and more difficult to discriminate between useful and useless information. (p. 356)

T _____ 36. Researchers have found that e-mail is the greatest contributor to information overload. (p. 357)

F _____ 37. "Information architects" are designers who help companies determine office layouts that are optimal for employee comfort. (p. 357)

T _____ 38. The existence of the Internet and intranets has posed significant security threats for business organizations. (p. 358)

T _____ 39. Employers have the legal right to monitor employee e-mail and voice-mail messages. (p. 359)

F _____ 40. Both e-mail and voice mail are inadmissible as evidence in court cases. (p. 359)

MULTIPLE CHOICE

b _____ 1. Telecommuting links people who work at home, in a suburban satellite office, and on the road by using (p. 338)
   a. overnight delivery services.
   b. computers, phones, and faxes.
   c. memos, letters, and reports.
   d. all of the above.

a _____ 2. A disadvantage of recent advances in communication technology is that (p. 338)
   a. they have blurred the line between work life and home life.
   b. they are more expensive than traditional communications methods.
   c. they are making changes in the workplace.
   d. all of the above.

c _____ 3. The world's largest network of many electronically connected computers is (p. 339)
   a. the LAN.
   b. the WAN.
   c. the Internet.
   d. the Extranet.

b _____ 4. A Web site's unique address is called a (p. 339)
   a. hypertext transfer protocol.
   b. uniform resource locator.
   c. home page.
   d. server address.

a _____   5.   Telnet is (p. 340)
   a.   a class of Internet application programs that allow you to connect with a remote host even though your computer is not part of the network that host supports.
   b.   a secured intranet area.
   c.   a way for Internet users to converse vocally.
   d.   a proprietary browser used for accessing the World Wide Web.

c _____   6.   Which of the following is *not* an advantage of e-mail? (pp. 341–342)
   a.   It delivers messages almost instantaneously.
   b.   It is low in cost.
   c.   It helps to reduce information overload.
   d.   It is egalitarian.

.b _____   7.   A method that allows individuals in different locations to speak together in real time and share documents electronically is (p. 342)
   a.   Usenet newsgroups.
   b.   videoconferencing.
   c.   listservs.
   d.   voice recognition.

a _____   8.   A system that allows you to download files from the Internet and upload files as well is (p. 343)
   a.   FTP.
   b.   PBX.
   c.   DSL.
   d.   WDM.

d _____   9.   A discussion group that you subscribe to via e-mail is called a (p. 344)
   a.   Usenet newsgroup.
   b.   distribution list.
   c.   directory.
   d.   listserv.

a _____   10.   A discussion group that you visit at a site where individuals can read and post messages is called a (p. 344)
   a.   Usenet newsgroup.
   b.   distribution list.
   c.   directory.
   d.   listserv.

c _____   11.   A live online conversation in real time is called a (p. 344)
   a.   Usenet newsgroup.
   b.   distribution list.
   c.   chat.
   d.   listserv.

a _____ 12. A search engine (pp. 344–345)
    a. travels the Web automatically, looking for new Web pages to add to its database.
    b. uses humans to conduct its Web searches.
    c. does not include Usenet newsgroups in its database.
    d. all of the above.

b _____ 13. If you use different search engines (p. 345)
    a. you will pretty much get identical results.
    b. you will find that some only index the most popular Web pages.
    c. you can use the same search methods for each one.
    d. you will be wasting your time.

d _____ 14. Directories differ from search engines in that (p. 345)
    a. they are primarily metacrawlers.
    b. they index only the most popular Web pages.
    c. they index primarily Usenet newsgroups.
    d. they use human beings instead of automated software to handle their indexing.

b _____ 15. Getting information by using a search engine is an example of (p. 347)
    a. push technology.
    b. pull technology.
    c. telecommuting.
    d. intranetting.

a _____ 16. A personal agent is (p. 348)
    a. a type of push technology in which software agents mold your desktop information to your personal interests.
    b. a type of handheld computer.
    c. someone who advises individuals about their hardware and software needs.
    d. a type of search engine.

b _____ 17. A private corporate network that connects computers within a company is called a(n) (p. 348)
    a. personal agent.
    b. intranet.
    c. firewall.
    d. listserv.

c _____ 18. A firewall is a (p. 348)
    a. type of virus protection software.
    b. Web site for flamers.
    c. special type of gateway that control's access to an intranet.
    d. threat to intranet security.

d _____ 19. Which of the following is *not* an advantage of an intranet? (p. 349)
   a. All company computers can link to it, even if they have different operating systems.
   b. It enables employees at different sites to collaborate with one another.
   c. It saves the company time and money.
   d. They provide personal agents to each user.

c _____ 20. If a company creates an intranet (pp. 351–352)
   a. employees can be expected to flock to it.
   b. it can be expected to organize information for the company.
   c. information systems should be moved onto the intranet gradually.
   d. all of the above.

a _____ 21. An organized network that allows outsiders to have limited access to an intranet is called (p. 352)
   a. an extranet.
   b. a listserv.
   c. a WAN.
   d. a firewall.

b _____ 22. A call-management system is (p. 353)
   a. a type of voice mail.
   b. is a computerized business phone system that gives companies control over both incoming and outgoing calls.
   c. a way to screen incoming phone calls to avoid solicitors.
   d. a wireless phone system being tried by some businesses.

d _____ 23. The market for wireless phones in the United States has been held back by (pp. 353)
   a. incompatible technologies.
   b. high user costs.
   c. failure to adopt the "caller pays" system.
   d. all of the above.

c _____ 24. Which of the following is *not* an advantage of voice mail? (p. 355)
   a. It allows you to review your messages before sending them.
   b. It reduces a substantial amount of interoffice paperwork.
   c. It keeps you from having to speak to the person you're trying to reach.
   d. It makes it easier to communicate with people in other time zones.

a _____ 25. Speech-recognition software (pp. 356–357)
   a. is used with voice-mail systems.
   b. is virtually error-free under just about any conditions.
   c. grasps context as well as words.
   d. does all of the above.

b _____ 26. The amount of information workers are receiving in the Information Age (pp. 356-357)
   a. still hasn't reach the human capacity for processing it.
   b. is causing information overload.
   c. has reached its peak and is starting to subside.
   d. allows them to make better decisions about what to pay attention to.

d _____ 27. The greatest contributor to information overload is (p. 357)
     a. faxes.
     b. voice mail.
     c. regular phone calls.
     d. e-mail.

c _____ 28. Companies hire information architects to (p. 357)
     a. design more comfortable workspaces for computer users.
     b. reconfigure their Web browsers.
     c. to reorganize company information into more effective communication.
     d. construct their Web sites.

d _____ 29. About what percentage of companies have suffered financial losses as a result of breaches in computer security? (p. 359)
     a. 5 percent
     b. 15 percent
     c. 35 percent
     d. 75 percent

b _____ 30. When it comes to employee productivity, use of the Internet has been shown to (p. 359)
     a. have no effect on employee productivity.
     b. decrease employee productivity because of misuse of the Internet.
     c. increase employee productivity because of the immediate access to desired information.
     d. increase employee productivity because it eliminates the need to use other forms of communication.

FILL-INS

1. People who work away from the office through computers, phones, and faxes are _____. (p. 328)

2. The _____ is the world's largest network of electronically connected computers. (p. 339)

3. The _____ _____ _____ is a portion of the Internet that allows for graphics, sound, and video. (p. 339)

4. The _____ _____ of a Web site is the primary screen that visitors first see when visiting the site. (p. 339)

5. Each Web site is identified by a unique address known as an URL, or _____ _____ _____. (p. 339)

6. _____ is a class of Internet application programs that allow you to connect with a remote host even though your computer is not a permanent part of the network your host supports. (p. 340)

7. Using _____, anybody can send messages to just about anybody else, which increases the communication between lower-level employees and upper-level management. (p. 341)

8. With FTP, or _____ _____ _____, you can download files from the Internet, as well as upload them to the Internet. (p. 343)

9. A discussion mailing list, or _____, is an e-mail discussion group to which you subscribe. (p. 344)

10. A _____ _____ travels the World Wide Web looking for new Web sites to place in a database called an index or a catalog. (p. 344)

11. Whereas a search engine uses automated software to find Web sites, a _____ uses humans to do this job. (p. 345)

12. An _____ is a private corporate network that connects company computers in various locations. (p. 348)

13. An _____ allows prequalified outsiders to have access to a company's intranet. (p. 352)

14. To better control phone calls, both incoming and outgoing, some organizations rely on a _____ _____ system. (p. 353)

ANSWERS

1.	telecommuting	8.	file transfer protocol
2.	Internet	9.	listserv
3.	World Wide Web	10.	search engine
4.	home page	11.	directory
5.	uniform resource locator	12.	intranet
6.	Telnet	13.	extranet
7.	e-mail	14.	call-management

CHAPTER 11
FINDING, EVALUATING, AND PROCESSING INFORMATION

TRUE OR FALSE

T _____ 1. The best way to learn about something new is to browse through materials on the topic. (p. 368)

F _____ 2. If you are researching a complex problem, the best approach is to start by gathering as many materials about it as possible from as many sources as possible. (p. 370)

F _____ 3. You need to prepare a preliminary outline for a study only if the person authorizing the study specifically requests it. (p. 370)

F _____ 4. When preparing an outline for a study, you should always use the alphanumeric system. (p. 370)

F _____ 5. An example of a descriptive (topical) outline heading would be "Profit margins are narrow." (p. 370)

T _____ 6. Informative outlines take longer to write but are generally more helpful than descriptive outlines. (p. 370)

T _____ 7. Reference books, journal articles, and past reports are all examples of secondary research sources. (p. 372)

T _____ 8. Electronic databases are available on CD-ROM as well as online. (p. 373)

F _____ 9. When you need to consult government documents, you go to the appropriate government office in your city. (pp. 373–374)

F _____ 10. When using the Internet to conduct research, you can be reasonably sure that any information you find will be accurate. (p. 374)

T _____ 11. To conduct an effective database search on the Web, you should use multiple search engines. (p. 376)

F _____ 12. If you were researching how to invest in Web-based companies, you would type "How to Invest in Web-based Companies" in the search prompt. (p. 376)

T _____ 13. You can improve your database search results by using Boolean operators. (p. 377)

T _____ 14. Observation, surveys, and experiments are all types of primary research. (p. 379)

T _____ 15. A single document may be both a primary and a secondary source. (p. 379)

F _____ 16.   Because observation is such an unreliable research method, it has little to offer when it comes to business studies. (p. 379)

T _____ 17.   An interview with an expert is the simplest form of survey. (p. 379)

T _____ 18.   A survey is considered valid if it measures what it is intended to measure. (p. 379)

F _____ 19.   Because surveys produce varying results according to how questions are worded and which people are surveyed, they are a poor form of research. (pp. 379–380)

T _____ 20.   When preparing a questionnaire, you should pretest it on a sample group to identify any questions that might be misinterpreted. (p. 380)

F _____ 21.   If you enclose a preaddressed, stamped envelope with a questionnaire, you can expect a response rate of about 50 percent. (p. 380)

F _____ 22.   An interview is an easy way to get information about a topic, and it requires very little preparation and time. (p. 381)

T _____ 23.   When conducting an interview, you should use a mix of interview questions, including open-ended, closed-ended, and restatement questions. (p. 383)

F _____ 24.   It's better for interviews to take place in person than to conduct them via e-mail. (p. 384)

T _____ 25.   After you have gathered research materials, the next step is to evaluate the usefulness of the information and the credibility of your sources. (p. 384)

F _____ 26.   You should not use any information provided by organizations that have a distinct bias, such as the Tobacco Institute or the American Association of Retired Persons. (p. 385)

T _____ 27.   You can stop your research process when you have answered all your basic questions and your efforts are yielding little new information. (p. 386)

F _____ 28.   Making notes about research materials is one area where computers aren't very helpful. (p. 387)

T _____ 29.   If you use note cards for research information, you should make separate cards for each fact, quotation, or general concept you want to record. (p. 387)

T _____ 30.   You should avoid using too many direct quotations in your reports. (p. 387)

F _____ 31.   A good paraphrase should be the same length as or slightly longer than the original passage. (p. 389)

T _____ 32.   Even if you paraphrase material, it's best to give credit to the source you obtained the original information from. (p. 389)

F _____ 33.   Titles and slogans can be copyrighted. (p. 389)

T _____ 34. According to the fair use doctrine, you can use other people's work only as long as you do not unfairly prevent them from benefiting as a result. (p. 389)

T _____ 35. The raw statistical information you gather for your report is of little value until you manipulate it. (p. 391)

F _____ 36. If sales for the first six months of the year were $24,000, $20,000, $23,000, $20,000, $19,000, and $21,000, the mean for the six months would be $20,000. (p. 391)

T _____ 37. The median is a useful average when one or a few of the numbers in a group is extreme. (p. 391)

T _____ 38. The mode is the number that occurs most often in a set of figures. (p. 391)

T _____ 39. When analyzing data, it is usually useful to look at findings over time in order to detect patterns and relationships. (p. 391)

F _____ 40. If you find a strong correlation between company stress-reduction programs and increased worker productivity, you can conclude that such programs do indeed cause increased productivity. (p. 392)

MULTIPLE CHOICE

c _____ 1. When embarking on a research project, the first thing you need to do is (p. 378)
    a. gather together all your research materials.
    b. go to the library.
    c. identify the main question you are trying to answer.
    d. surf the World Wide Web.

d _____ 2. You may not need a detailed preliminary outline if (p. 378)
    a. several other people are working on the assignment.
    b. the investigation will be extensive.
    c. the assignment might be revised during the investigation.
    d. the report will be short and informal.

b _____ 3. The headings in an outline are usually (p. 370)
    a. in descriptive form.
    b. in parallel form.
    c. in topical form.
    d. complete statements.

c _____ 4. Which of the following is an example of a descriptive outline heading? (pp. 370)
    a. What is the Nature of the Industry?
    b. Flour Milling Is a Mature Industry
    c. The Flour Milling Industry
    d. Sales Growth in the Industry Is Slow

a _____ 5.   Once you've defined the problem and prepared an outline, your next step is to (p. 371)
   a.   identify the best sources of information to use for your research.
   b.   prepare a questionnaire.
   c.   start writing information on notecards.
   d.   determine preliminary conclusions and recommendations.

d _____ 6.   Which of the following is *not* a secondary source of information? (p. 372)
   a.   books in the library
   b.   magazine and journal articles
   c.   Web pages
   d.   questionnaires

c _____ 7.   An example of a secondary research source for a report about whether to publish a company newsletter would be (p. 372)
   a.   interviews with editors of newsletters at other companies.
   b.   an estimate from a printer on what it would cost to print a newsletter.
   c.   a magazine article on the pros and cons of company newsletters.
   d.   a survey of employees to determine their interest in a newsletter.

a _____ 8.   If you are searching for information about a specific industry, it's a good idea to know (p. 374)
   a.   its SIC and/or NAICS code.
   b.   how to use Boolean operators.
   c.   whether companies in that industry tend to be private or publicly traded.
   d.   some names of people who work in that industry.

d _____ 9.   If you use the Internet to research a company, keep in mind that (p. 376)
   a.   it may not have a Web site.
   b.   if the information you're looking for exists on the Web, you still may not be able to find it.
   c.   search engines will probably turn up a lot of information you don't need.
   d.   all of the above.

b _____ 10. To conduct an effective database search (pp. 376–377)
   a.   choose one search engine and stick with it.
   b.   enter variations of your search terms to increase the likelihood of obtaining desirable "hits."
   c.   use long search phrases rather than short ones or single terms.
   d.   avoid Boolean operators.

c _____ 11. If you wanted to find information about Portland, Oregon hotels in a database, the best Boolean search strategy would be (p. 377)
   a.   Portland hotels.
   b.   Portland AND hotels.
   c.   Portland AND hotels NOT Maine.
   d.   Portland AND hotels NOT Maine NOT motels OR bed-and-breakfasts.

b _____ 12. Which of these documents would *not* usually qualify as primary research? (p. 379)
    a. a sales report from a company rep
    b. the most recent issue of a trade magazine in your industry
    c. correspondence with a particular customer
    d. your company's latest balance sheet

d _____ 13. Using formal observation to obtain data is (p. 379)
    a. too subjective to be useful in business research.
    b. useful primarily for studies in which variables can be manipulated.
    c. usually more reliable than other research methods.
    d. useful for studying physical activities, the environment, or human behavior.

a _____ 14. Survey results are considered reliable when (p. 379)
    a. similar results would be obtained if the survey were repeated.
    b. a representative group of people has been surveyed.
    c. the research measures what it was intended to measure.
    d. the phrasing of the questions is unbiased.

c _____ 15. Survey results are considered valid when (p. 379)
    a. similar results would be obtained if the survey were repeated.
    b. a representative group of people has been surveyed.
    c. the research measures what it was intended to measure.
    d. the phrasing of the questions is unbiased.

a _____ 16. People are more likely to respond to a questionnaire if (p. 380)
    a. they can complete it within 10 or 15 minutes.
    b. you allow them plenty of time to research their answers.
    c. the questions are open ended.
    d. all of the above.

d _____ 17. To help obtain valid results from a questionnaire, you (p. 380)
    a. ask mostly compound questions.
    b. use abstract terminology.
    c. include questions that lead to the particular answers you are seeking.
    d. formulate questions for which answers can be easily tabulated or analyzed.

c _____ 18. When preparing to conduct an interview (p. 382)
    a. you need to take into account the interviewee's cultural and language background.
    b. it is helpful to get the questions to the interviewee a day or two ahead of time.
    c. organize the interview to have an opening, a body, and a close.
    d. all of the above.

b _____ 19. When conducting an interview (p. 383)
    a. stick to asking only one type of question.
    b. ask the most important questions first.
    c. try to get in as many questions as possible, even if the interview will run over the allotted time.
    d. avoid using direct open-ended questions.

c _____ 20.   The value of your report depends most strongly on (p. 384)
  a.   the number of sources you have consulted.
  b.   the depth to which you have covered the topic.
  c.   the quality of the information on which the report is based.
  d.   the importance of the research.

a _____ 21.   When taking notes on your research material (p. 387)
  a.   for each note record source information or supply a cross-reference to bibliography cards.
  b.   avoid trying to use computer programs for this task, as they get in the way more than they help.
  c.   you do not need to include subject headings.
  d.   try to fit as many facts as possible on each card.

b _____ 22.   To paraphrase effectively (pp. 388–389)
  a.   avoid using any business language or jargon..
  b.   double-check your version against the original to make sure that you haven't altered the meaning.
  c.   make sure your version is the same length as or longer than the original.
  d.   do all of the above.

d _____ 23.   You would not need to cite a source if you (p. 389)
  a.   used a direct quotation of under 250 words from a book titled *Modern Economics.*
  b.   used a table from *The 1985 Farmer's Almanac.*
  c.   described, in your own words, a plan for organizing production lines, which appeared in a professional journal.
  d.   made several observations about the market for soft drinks, confirmed by several articles in the popular press.

b _____ 24.   You would need to write for permission if you wanted to directly quote (p. 389)
  a.   two paragraphs of 175 words total from a book titled *Modern Economics.*
  b.   three lines from the song "Takin' Care of Business."
  c.   six pages from *Patents and Trademarks*, a pamphlet from the U.S. Government Printing Office.
  d.   ten poems by Edgar Allan Poe.

a _____ 25.   The most commonly used average is the (p. 391)
  a.   mean.
  b.   median.
  c.   mode.
  d.   correlation.

b _____ 26.   What would be the median for the following set of monthly salaries: $1200, $1200, $1300, $1500, $1700, $2000, $2800? (p. 391)
  a. $1200
  b. $1500
  c. $1671.43
  d. $1700

c _____ 27. In a particular set of figures or data, the number that occurs most often is called the (p. 391)
- a. mean.
- b. median.
- c. mode.
- d. correlation.

a _____ 28. Trend analysis involves (p. 391)
- a. examining data over a period of time in order to detect patterns and relationships.
- b. examining the statistical relationship that exists between two or more variables.
- c. calculating the mean, median, mode, and range for a set of data.
- d. all of the above.

d _____ 29. Once you have identified a trend, you (p. 392)
- a. can draw conclusions and make recommendations.
- b. can make a positive correlation between variables.
- c. can prove a cause-and-effect relationship.
- d. need to establish the cause.

d _____ 30. If you find that Gary Harper consistently sells the most electronic keyboards in your music store, you can conclude that (p. 392)
- a. he is your best salesperson.
- b. he knows more about electronic keyboards than any other salesperson.
- c. he is more aggressive than the other salespeople.
- d. none of the above.

FILL-INS

1. To begin your research project, start with a _____ _____ that defines the purpose of your research. (p. 370)

2. You can organize your study by preparing a preliminary _____. (p. 370)

3. When doing research, you use both _____ resources (those that provide firsthand information) and _____ resources (secondhand reports). (p. 371)

4. An electronic _____ is a computer-searchable collection of information. (p. 373)

5. When conducting a database search, you use _____. _____ or search terms, to narrow down your search. (p. 376)

6. Using _____ _____ such as AND, OR, and NOT can help you in your database searches. (p. 377)

7. The aim in conducting _____ is to keep all variables the same except for the one you are testing. (p. 379)

8. A survey is considered _____ when the same results would be obtained if the research were repeated. (p. 379)

9. A survey is considered _____ when it measures what it was intended to measure. (p. 379)

10. When conducting an interview, you use _____ questions to get the interviewee to offer an opinion and not just a yes-or-no answer. (p. 383)

11. Instead of using long direct quotes from sources, you should try to _____ the material. (p. 387)

12. The most commonly used average is the _____, or the sum of all the items in the group divided by the total number of items. (p. 391)

13. Examining data over time to detect patterns and relationships is called _____ _____. (p. 391)

14. A _____ is a statistical relationship between two or more variables. (p. 392)

ANSWERS

1. problem statement
2. outline
3. primary, secondary
4. database
5. key words
6. Boolean operators
7. experiments

8. reliable
9. valid
10. open-ended
11. paraphrase
12. mean
13. trend analysis
14. correlation

CHAPTER 12
COMMUNICATING INFORMATION
THROUGH GRAPHS AND OTHER VISUALS

TRUE OR FALSE

T _____ 1. When they begin the composition phase of a report, many experienced businesspeople start with the visual aids. (p. 400)

F _____ 2. Although visual aids attract and hold people's attention, they don't help comprehension or retention of a message. (p. 400)

T _____ 3. Meetings involving graphic presentations have been found to be shorter than those without graphics. (p. 400)

F _____ 4. Visual aids are so useful in getting ideas across to an audience that businesspeople can feel free to use illustrative material in great quantity. (p. 400)

T _____ 5. One way to approach the selection of visual aids is to think of each of your major points as a separate scene. (p. 401)

F _____ 6. Most topics require about the same number of visual aids. (p. 402)

F _____ 7. It's a good idea to use a chart, table, or graph to illustrate every point in a written report. (p. 402)

F _____ 8. Once you know what point you want to present visually, you will automatically know what format to choose. (p. 402)

T _____ 9. Tables are ideal for summarizing information that would be difficult or tedious to handle in the main text. (p. 403)

T _____ 10. Every table includes vertical columns and horizontal rows. (p. 403)

T _____ 11. It is all right to present a table sideways on a page if it has too many columns to fit upright. (p. 403)

F _____ 12. Word tables are not as useful as numerical ones. (p. 403)

F _____ 13. In line charts showing trends, the vertical axis indicates time or quantity, and the horizontal axis indicates amount. (p. 404)

F _____ 14. If at all possible, use no more than six lines on any given line chart. (p. 404)

F _____ 15. A surface chart is a type of bar chart in which the bars are represented by symbols. (p. 405)

F _____ 16.   Bar charts have limited use because they can only be used to compare two sets of data. (p. 405)

T _____ 17.   The chief value of pictograms is their novelty. (p. 407)

T _____ 18.   A Gantt chart is a type of timeline chart that helps track progress on a project. (p. 408)

T _____ 19.   Pie charts are a good way of illustrating the composition of a whole. (p. 408)

T _____ 20.   When you are preparing a pie chart, you limit the number of slices in the pie to no more than seven. (p. 408)

T _____ 21.   If you want to illustrate a process or procedure, the best type of visual aid to use is the flow chart. (p. 409)

T _____ 22.   An organization's normal communication channels are almost impossible to describe without the use of an organization chart. (p. 409)

F _____ 23.   The visual aids most commonly used in business reports are drawings, diagrams, and photographs. (p. 410)

F _____ 24.   Because of the costs of reproduction, photographs are not used in business reports. (p. 413)

T _____ 25.   Thanks to improved technology, it is now possible for businesspeople to produce high-quality visual aids without the services of graphic designers. (p. 413)

T _____ 26.   The image you want to project determines your production technique. (p. 415)

T _____ 27.   Most people subconsciously recognize good design when they see it. (p. 416)

F _____ 28.   Making arbitrary changes in color, shape, size, or texture is one way of stimulating an audience's interest in your presentation. (p. 416)

T _____ 28.   Audiences expect visual distinctions to match verbal distinctions. (p. 416)

T _____ 30.   Audiences assume that the most important point will receive the most visual emphasis. (p. 416)

T _____ 31   The best time to consider the principles of good design is before preparing visual aids; making changes after the fact increases their production time. (p. 416)

T _____ 32.   In the text of a report, every visual aid is clearly referred to by number. (p. 418)

T _____ 33.   The best place to put a visual aid is right next to or immediately following the paragraph it illustrates. (p. 418)

T _____ 34.   One of the best ways to tie your visual aids to the text is to choose titles and captions that reinforce the point you are trying to make. (p. 419)

F _____ 35.   When writing titles for illustrations, you can make some of them descriptive and some of them informative, depending on the type of visual. (p. 419)

T _____ 36.   Audiences remember only 10 percent of a speaker's message when it is presented solely through words, but they remember 50 percent when the information is supported with visuals such as slides. (p. 422–423)

Y _____ 37.   Presentation software allows you to incorporate multimedia such as sound and video into a presentation. (p. 424)

F _____ 38.   All handouts should be distributed prior to a speech or presentation. (p. 424)

F _____ 39.   When building an electronic presentation, you design each slide to include several points or visuals. (p. 425)

T _____ 40.   As a rule of thumb, text visuals for presentations should consist of no more than six lines, with a maximum of six words per line. (p. 428)

MULTIPLE CHOICE

a _____ 1.   Visual aids are useful to business professionals because (p. 400)
   a.   in our number-oriented work world, people rely heavily on visual images.
   b.   they are quicker and cheaper than developing text.
   c.   they allow speakers to lengthen their presentations considerably.
   d.   they take the place of having to provide any verbal information.

b _____ 2.   The first step in composing a report or presentation is (p. 401)
   a.   getting the "go ahead" from your supervisor.
   b.   deciding on the message.
   c.   deciding on the graphics.
   d.   deciding on the length.

a _____ 3.   The ideal balance between the visual and the verbal depends on (p. 402)
   a.   the nature of the subject being discussed.
   b.   the length of the report/presentation.
   c.   the amount of money available for underwriting the costs of graphics.
   d.   internal company guidelines.

b _____ 4.   When you develop individual visual aids for your report or presentation, you (p. 402)
   a.   choose the least costly graphics.
   b.   choose the specific form that best suits your message.
   c.   choose primarily text visuals rather than graphic visuals.
   d.   do all of the above.

a _____ 5.   If you have a great deal of factual information to present, it would be best to (p. 403)
    a. use a table.
    b. use a pie chart.
    c. use a diagram.
    d. put it all in the main body of the report.

c _____ 6.   When preparing a table, keep in mind that (pp. 403–404)
    a. it should never be turned sideways.
    b. tabular materials should not be included within the text proper.
    c. all items in a column should be expressed in the same units.
    d. all of the above.

c _____ 7.   The best type of visual aid for showing trends over time is (p. 404)
    a. a table.
    b. a pie chart.
    c. a line chart.
    d. an organization chart.

c _____ 8.   In a line chart, using an axis with both positive and negative numbers is (p. 404)
    a. always confusing to your audience.
    b. best restricted to reports aimed at sophisticated audiences.
    c. handy when you have to illustrate losses.
    d. preferable to using a pie chart.

b _____ 9.   A surface chart is (p. 405)
    a. a type of three-dimensional pie chart.
    b. a form of line chart in which all the lines add up to the top line.
    c. a type of map showing various terrains.
    d. used to show interrelationships within an organization.

b _____ 10.   A bar chart would be particularly useful for (p. 405)
    a. summarizing the salaries of presidents at 20 corporations from 1987 to 1990.
    b. comparing market shares of three breakfast cereals from 1987 to 1990.
    c. showing the stages in production of a jet engine.
    d. depicting the proportion of advertising dollars spent on various major media.

a _____ 11.   Bar charts can be converted into (p. 407)
    a. pictograms.
    b. flow charts.
    c. organization charts.
    d. surface charts.

a _____ 12.   The best way to illustrate the composition of a whole is with a (p. 408)
    a. pie chart.
    b. line chart.
    c. bar chart.
    d. flow chart.

b _____ 13. When preparing a pie chart, you (p. 408)
    a. limit the number of slices to no more than three.
    b. place the largest segment at the 12 o'clock position.
    c. arrange wedges of decreasing importance in a counterclockwise direction.
    d. do all of the above.

d _____ 14. Flowcharts are used to (p. 409)
    a. summarize large amounts of statistical data.
    b. show the relative sizes of the parts of a whole.
    c. show how something looks or operates.
    d. illustrate processes and procedures.

b _____ 15. One of the most common uses of maps in business reports is (p. 409)
    a. to show physical differences in variables.
    b. to show concentrations of variables by geographic area.
    c. to show quality differences in variables.
    d. to show business locations.

b _____ 16. Drawings, diagrams, and photographs are (p. 410)
    a. commonly used in business reports.
    b. occasionally used in business reports.
    c. never used in business reports.
    d. used in oral presentations but not in written reports.

c _____ 17. A photograph is especially useful for (p. 413)
    a. showing progression over time.
    b. showing cumulative effects.
    c. demonstrating the exact appearance of a new product.
    d. showing how the parts relate to the whole.

a _____ 18. Producing visual aids with a computer-graphics system is (p. 413)
    a. a way to cut both costs and time.
    b. cost-efficient but still labor-intensive.
    c. not advisable unless you have access to extremely expensive computer equipment.
    d. not likely to result in professional-looking materials.

d _____ 19. One of the great advantages of spreadsheet programs is that (p. 413)
    a. they communicate a subtle message about your relationship with the audience.
    b. they determine for you the appropriate way to fit your visual aids into your text.
    c. they are cheap.
    d. they are both an analytical tool and a communication tool.

c _____ 20. Making arbitrary changes in the color, size, or shape of your visual aids may (p. 416)
    a. stimulate the flagging interest of your audience.
    b. be difficult to do without sophisticated software or the help of a graphic designer.
    c. confuse your audience.
    d. unnecessarily lengthen your report/presentation.

a _____ 21.   An audience assumes that the most important point will (p. 416)
    a.   receive the most visual emphasis.
    b.   be repeated three times by the speaker/writer.
    c.   be obvious.
    d.   be stated in the first few sentences of the report or presentation.

d _____ 22.   An audience expects that visual distinctions will (p. 416)
    a.   be repeated at least twice during the presentation.
    b.   be made at the beginning of the presentation.
    c.   be made at the end of the presentation.
    d.   match verbal distinctions.

b _____ 23.   How text and visual aids are integrated depends on (p. 418)
    a.   the type of computer software you used to generate the graphics.
    b.   the type of report you are preparing.
    c.   the overall length of your report.
    d.   the quality of the graphics.

a _____ 24.   You refer to each visual aid in your text by (p. 418)
    a.   number.
    b.   letter.
    c.   a combination of numbers and letters.
    d.   describing it.

b _____ 25.   A reference to a visual aid (p. 418)
    a.   comes directly after the piece itself appears.
    b.   precedes the piece itself.
    c.   comes fairly close to the appearance of the piece.
    d.   can appear anywhere as long as the piece is well-labeled.

c _____ 26.   If your visual aids are on separate sheets of paper, it's best to (p. 419)
    a.   cluster them at the end of each chapter.
    b.   insert them prior to the pages that refer to them.
    c.   insert them directly after the page that refers to them.
    d.   cluster them at the end of the report.

c _____ 27.   Legends are generally written as (p. 419)
    a.   short, one- or two-word descriptions.
    b.   descriptive phrases.
    c.   one or more complete sentences.
    d.   any of the above.

d _____ 28.   Which of the following is an example of a descriptive title for a visual aid? (p. 419)
    a.   How CamCo Reduces Costs
    b.   How Cost Reductions Have Been Made at CamCo
    c.   Reducing Costs Is a Number-One Goal at CamCo
    d.   CamCo Cuts Costs Through Outsourcing and Downsizing

a _____ 29. When using overhead transparencies in a presentation, keep in mind that (pp. 424–425)
   a. you can use special markers to write on them.
   b. they require a great deal of preparation.
   c. they require you to dim the lights
   d. you aren't able to face the audience.

b _____ 30. When building an electronic presentation, you should (pp. 425–427)
   a. disregard any templates that come with the software program.
   b. design each slide to cover one point or one graph.
   c. prepare them in the exact order in which they will appear, since it is very difficult to rearrange the order once you've completed all the slides
   d. keep in mind that presentation software is limited in its capabilities, so you will need to prepare handouts, speaker's notes, and outlines with other software packages.

FILL-INS

1. Tables, graphs, schematic drawings, and photographs are examples of _____
    _____. (p. 399)

2. A _____ is a type of visual aid that includes vertical columns and horizontal rows. (p. 403)

3. A _____ chart, or graph, illustrates trends over time. (p. 403)

4. _____ charts are a form of line chart with a cumulative effect; all the lines add up to the top line. (p. 405)

5. A _____ chart is a special type of timeline that tracks progress toward completion of a project. (p. 408)

6. Nothing is better for showing the composition of a whole than a _____ chart. (p. 408)

7. A _____ illustrates a sequence of events. (p. 409)

8. To illustrate the positions, units, or functions of an organization and the way they interrelate, use an _____ chart. (p. 409)

9. _____ and drawings are most often used to show how something looks or operates. (p. 410)

10. _____-_____ systems help cut the time and costs associated with preparing visual aids. (p. 413)

11. Line, mass, space, color, size, pattern, and texture are elements of _____ _____. (p. 416)

12. A(n) _____ title on a graphic simply identifies the topic, while a(n) _____ title calls attention to the conclusion that ought to be drawn from the data. (p. 419)

13. You can use large sheets of paper attached at the top, called _____, to illustrate points in a presentation. (p. 424)

14. Software packages such as PowerPoint are used to create an _____ _____, a series of computerized slides. (p. 425)

ANSWERS

1. visual aids
2. table
3. line
4. surface
5. Gantt
6. pie
7. flowchart
8. organization
9. diagrams
10. computer-graphics
11. graphic design
12. descriptive, informative
13. flip charts
14. electronic presentation

CHAPTER 13
COMMUNICATING THROUGH REPORTS

TRUE OR FALSE

T _____ 1. A business report is any factual, objective document that communicates information about some aspect of business. (p. 440)

T _____ 2. As you make decisions about report content, the needs of your audience are your main concern. (p. 440)

T _____ 3. When writing a voluntary (rather than an authorized) report, you need to provide more background on the subject and explain your purpose more carefully. (pp. 441–442)

T _____ 4. Routine reports submitted on a repeat basis are often prepared on preprinted forms. (pp. 442)

F _____ 5. External reports of fewer than ten pages are usually in memo format. (p. 442)

F _____ 6. Informational reports are usually organized to highlight conclusions, recommendations, or reasons. (p. 442)

F _____ 7. Analytical reports are primarily intended to educate readers. (p. 442)

T _____ 8. In an analytical report, facts are a means to an end rather than an end in themselves. (p. 442)

T _____ 9. One of the most common applications for business reports is to monitor and control the operations of the organization. (p. 442)

T _____ 10. If you are new in an organization, you use similar reports on file as a model for preparing monitor/control reports. (p. 442)

F _____ 11. A "marketing plan" and a "business plan" are the same thing. (p. 443)

T _____ 12. Management information systems are either computerized or manual systems that provide statistics on company operations and performance. (p. 443)

F _____ 13. Examples of operating reports are performance reviews, recruiting reports, and sales-call reports. (p. 444)

T _____ 14. A memo summarizing an employee's trip to a trade show would be an example of a personal activity report. (p. 444)

F _____ 15. Personal activity reports are normally written in letter format. (p. 444)

T _____ 16. Reports that discuss policies and procedures help managers get the same information out to all employees. (p. 447)

F _____ 17. A report explaining a company policy or procedure covers any conceivable question that readers might have. (p. 447)

F _____ 18. Position papers spell out lasting guidelines on company policies and procedures. (p. 449)

F _____ 19. Compliance reports are a type of analytical report aimed at obtaining compliance from the report's target audience. (p. 449)

T _____ 20. Examples of compliance reports are income tax returns and annual reports to shareholders. (p. 449)

T _____ 21. Many companies use their annual reports as a public relations tool and put financial data in only part of the report. (p. 451)

F _____ 22. Reports that document client work are always easy to write, as they are straightforward and routine. (p. 451)

F _____ 23. Interim progress reports to clients are rarely needed. (p. 451)

T _____ 24. Final reports serve as a permanent record of what was accomplished on a project. (p. 451)

T _____ 25. Analytical reports help managers make major decisions. (p. 454)

T _____ 26. Problem-solving reports require a strong foundation of facts. (p. 454)

T _____ 27. Troubleshooting reports usually begin with some background information on the problem and then analyze alternative solutions. (p. 455)

F _____ 28. A justification report is an example of an informational report. (p. 456)

T _____ 29. A justification report is an internal report designed to persuade top management to approve a proposed investment or project. (p. 455)

T _____ 30. Proposals are attempts to get products, plans, or projects accepted by outside business or government clients. (p. 456)

T _____ 31. Proposals are legally binding and must be prepared with extreme care. (p. 456)

T _____ 32. Two basic types of sales proposal are solicited and unsolicited. (p. 456)

T _____ 33. An invitation to bid on a contract is called an RFP. (p. 457)

F _____ 34. Like solicited proposals, unsolicited proposals are always initiated with an RFP. (p. 459)

F _____ 35. Solicited proposals spend a great deal of time explaining why the client should take action. (p. 459)

T _____ 36.   Unsolicited proposals vary widely in form and length, depending on the nature of the product being sold. (p. 459)

T _____ 37.   It's acceptable for a summary report to have a few factual errors and minor typos, since this type of report is for routine internal use. (p. 462)

F _____ 38.   Report-writing software essentially writes your report for you. (p. 464)

F _____ 39.   Electronic reports save on speed and space, but they are more costly to produce than paper reports. (p. 464)

T _____ 40.   Despite their many advantages, electronic reports are not a cure-all for business communication problems (p. 463)

MULTIPLE CHOICE

c _____ 1.   The goal in developing a report is to (p. 440)
    a.   impress the reader.
    b.   provide as much information as possible.
    c.   make the information as clear and convenient as possible.
    d.   do all of the above.

b _____ 2.   Which of the following is *not* a typical reason for writing a report? (p. 440)
    a.   to monitor and control operations
    b.   to schedule a business meeting
    c.   to obtain new business or funding
    d.   to guide decisions on particular issues

c _____ 3.   The basic purpose of informational reports is (p. 442)
    a.   to persuade the audience to act.
    b.   to present recommendations and conclusions.
    c.   to educate readers.
    d.   to convince the reader of the soundness of your thinking.

b _____ 4.   The purpose of an analytical report is to (p. 442)
    a.   educate readers.
    b.   persuade readers to accept certain conclusions or recommendations.
    c.   state policies and procedures.
    d.   monitor and control business operations.

b _____ 5.   Monitor/control reports include (p. 442)
    a.   policies and procedures.
    b.   plans, operating reports, and personal activity reports.
    c.   solicited and unsolicited sales proposals.
    d.   research, justification, and troubleshooting reports.

d _____ 6.   Which of the following is not a type of written plan typically used in business? (p. 443)
   a.   Strategic plan
   b.   Marketing plan
   c.   Business plan
   d.   Summary plan

c _____ 7.   One way to provide management with raw statistical data about company operations is through a (p. 444)
   a.   personal activity report.
   b.   justification report.
   c.   computer printout.
   d.   staff performance report.

b _____ 8.   A periodic report (p. 444)
   a.   describes what occurred during a convention or conference.
   b.   describes what happened in a department or division over a period of time.
   c.   persuades top management to approve a project.
   d.   helps top management reach a decision.

b _____ 9.   An expense report is an example of (p. 444)
   a.   an interim report.
   b.   a personal activity report.
   c.   a position paper.
   d.   an operating report.

a _____ 10.   When writing reports to implement policies and procedures, your goal is to (p. 447)
   a.   communicate company standards to all employees.
   b.   answer every potential question a reader might have.
   c.   simplify company policies and procedures into one or two general points.
   d.   do all of the above

d _____ 11.   An example of a lasting guideline would be (pp. 448–449)
   a.   a memo from the head of personnel announcing a reimbursement program for employees who continue their education.
   b.   a memo from the head of production giving procedures for streamlining product assembly.
   c.   a memo from the office manager explaining how to reserve the conference room for special meetings.
   d.   all of the above.

b _____ 12.   A memo from an office manager on the need for extra security procedures because of burglaries in the area is an example of a (p. 449)
   a.   lasting guideline.
   b.   position paper.
   c.   bureaucratic overreaction.
   d.   final report.

b _____ 13. When you write a compliance report, it is especially important to be (p. 449)
    a. brief and numbers-oriented.
    b. honest, thorough, and accurate.
    c. computer literate.
    d. college educated.

c _____ 14. Compliance reports are generally required by (p. 449)
    a. parent companies.
    b. accounting departments.
    c. government agencies.
    d. marketing departments.

c _____ 15. When companies produce their annual reports (pp. 450–451)
    a. they leave out all the financial data and focus on the accomplishments of the previous year.
    b. many try to make the report interesting by using gimmicks.
    c. most now skip the print medium altogether and send their reports in electronically.
    d. they do so voluntarily.

a _____ 16. Reports documenting work for a client may be difficult to write if (p. 451)
    a. the work is not going well.
    b. you know the client's needs.
    c. the client makes few demands.
    d. the work is going very well.

c _____ 17. The purpose of an interim report is to (p. 451)
    a. give the final results of work.
    b. give the general plan of action for undertaking the client's request.
    c. give the client an idea of the work that has been accomplished to date.
    d. provide a basis for billing the client.

b _____ 18. Final reports differ from interim reports in that (p. 451)
    a. final reports are generally less elaborate than interim reports.
    b. final reports serve as a permanent record of what was accomplished.
    c. final reports deal primarily with how the work got done.
    d. final reports have no deadline and can be done at any time after the project is completed.

a _____ 19. In many ways, the most interesting business reports are (p. 454)
    a. decision-oriented ones.
    b. expense reports.
    c. annual financial statements.
    d. summaries of hiring policies.

b _____ 20. Despite the variety among them, all analytical reports tend to have (p. 454)
    a. a standard opening.
    b. a "should we or shouldn't we" quality.
    c. a "this is how it's done" quality.
    d. a standard middle section.

c _____ 21.   An internal report that investigates a problem and then offers a recommended
                 solution is the (p. 455)
                 a.   monitor/control report.
                 b.   business plan.
                 c.   troubleshooting report.
                 d.   interim progress report.

c _____ 22.   A justification report is (p. 456)
                 a.   an individual's daily description of what occurred during a convention or conference.
                 b.   an internal report that describes what has happened in a department or division during a
                      particular period.
                 c.   an internal proposal to persuade top management to approve a project.
                 d.   a decision-oriented document prepared for submission to top management.

a _____ 23.   Proposals, unlike justification reports, (p. 456)
                 a.   are legally binding.
                 b.   are internal as opposed to external reports.
                 c.   are always in memo format.
                 d.   do not require a great deal of supporting data.

b _____ 24.   Proposals differ from justification reports in that (p. 456)
                 a.   sales proposals are considerably longer than justification reports.
                 b.   sales proposals involve competition with other organizations and justification reports do
                      not.
                 c.   sales proposals are considerably shorter than justification reports.
                 d.   sales proposals are usually in memo form and justification reports are in letter form.

c _____ 25.   Solicited proposals are prepared (p. 457)
                 a.   by companies attempting to obtain business.
                 b.   by government regulatory agencies.
                 c.   by companies at the request of clients who need something done.
                 d.   by clients who wish to acquire the services of highly regarded companies.

b _____ 26.   It makes sense for a company to get several competing bids if (p. 459)
                 a.   it has limited funds and needs to find the cheapest supplier possible.
                 b.   it is spending a lot of money for the product or service it needs.
                 c.   it has a great deal of lead-time available for sifting through proposals.
                 d.   it is just starting out in a new market.

a _____ 27.   In an unsolicited proposal, the writer (p. 459)
                 a.   explains why the client should take action.
                 b.   analyzes the client's business in light of the competition.
                 c.   uses a style approved by the American Association of Business Writers.
                 d.   enumerates the client's options regarding such business decisions as product-line expan-
                      sion.

c _____ 28.   A business plan aimed at obtaining funds for a new venture is a type of (p. 459)
   a.   justification report.
   b.   solicited proposal.
   c.   unsolicited proposal.
   d.   troubleshooting report.

a _____ 29.   A good summary report is (p. 462)
   a.   comprehensive.
   b.   opinionated.
   c.   easy to write.
   d.   all of the above.

a _____ 30.   Which of the following is *not* an advantage of electronic reports? (p. 464)
   a.   They require little training in order to be created and sent.
   b.   They are easy to correct and update.
   c.   In the long run, they save money.
   d.   They allow for faster distribution.

FILL-INS

1.   A business _____ is a factual account that objectively communicates information about some aspect of the business. (p. 440)

2.   Voluntary reports require more detail and support than _____ reports, which are prepared at the request of another person. (p. 441)

3.   Whereas _____ reports focus on facts, _____ reports include interpretation, conclusions, and recommendations. (p. 442)

4.   Plans, operating reports, and personal activity reports are a few examples of reports that _____ and _____ an organization's operations. (p. 442)

5.   A common monitor/control report is the _____ , used to establish guidelines for future action. (p. 443)

6.   To gain information about operations, many managers use a _____ _____ _____ (MIS), which captures statistics about everything happening in an organization. (p. 443)

7.   A _____ _____ report is an individual's description of what occurred during a conference or a convention. (p. 444)

8.   In contrast to lasting policy/procedure reports, _____ _____ treat less permanent issues. (p. 449)

9.   All _____ reports are written in response to regulations of one sort or another. (p. 449)

10.   Interim _____ reports give others an idea of work that has been accomplished to date on a project. (p. 451)

11.   A _____ report gives the results of an investigation into a problem and offers a proposal for solution of the problem. (p. 455)

12.   A _____ report is an internal proposal used to persuade top management to approve an investment or a project. (p. 456)

13.   A(n) _____ proposal is initiated by a company that is trying to obtain business or funding on its own, without a specific offer from a client. (p. 459)

14.   A _____ report presents a distillation of information in one's own words. (p. 462)

ANSWERS

1.   report
2.   authorized
3.   informational, analytical
4.   monitor, control
5.   plan
6.   management information system
7.   personal activity

8.   position papers
9.   compliance
10.   progress
11.   troubleshooting
12.   justification
13.   unsolicited
14.   summary

CHAPTER 14
PLANNING, ORGANIZING, AND WRITING
REPORTS AND PROPOSALS

TRUE OR FALSE

T _____ 1. The first step in planning a long report is to define the problem. (p. 470)

T _____ 2. An effective way to limit the scope of your study is to use problem factoring. (p. 471)

F _____ 3. After you have defined the problem you will be investigating for a report, the next step is to begin your investigation. (p. 472)

T _____ 4. The way you outline an investigation may be different from the way you would outline the resulting report. (p. 472)

F _____ 5. The statement of purpose for a report is always presented as a question. (p. 472)

T _____ 6. After you've prepared a statement of purpose, it's a good idea to double-check it with the person who authorized the report. (p. 473)

F _____ 7. For any type of report, you need a formal work plan that outlines in detail each aspect of the proposed investigation. (p. 474)

T _____ 8. Conclusions are interpretations of what is meant by your evidence. (p. 475)

T _____ 9. You give recommendations in a report only if you've been asked to do so. (p. 477)

F _____ 10. An example of a recommendation would be "Given the slowdown in the real estate market and the past history of this particular property, it would not be a good acquisition at this time." (p. 477)

T _____ 11. If you make recommendations in your report, be certain that they are explained in enough detail for readers to take action. (p. 477)

T _____ 12. Recommendations in a report are of little use unless they are both practical and acceptable to the reader(s). (p. 477)

T _____ 13. When deciding on the content of your report, the first step is to put yourself in the audience's position. (p. 478)

F _____ 14. Using the indirect approach makes for a more forceful report that is particularly convenient to readers. (p. 479)

T _____ 15. The longer the report, the less effective the indirect approach is likely to be. (p. 480)

F _____ 16.   The direct and indirect approaches are never combined in a business report. (p. 480)

T _____ 17.   In general, the more routine the report, the less flexibility you have in deciding on format and length. (p. 480)

T _____ 18.   If a report to an outsider runs five or fewer pages, it can be presented in letter format. (p. 481)

F _____ 19.   Reports done in memo form do not include subheadings or visual aids. (p. 481)

F _____ 20.   Even when you are familiar with your readers, you should make your reports as long as possible in order to avoid any misunderstandings. (p. 482)

T _____ 21.   Short reports are more common in business than long ones. (p. 482)

T _____ 22.   A factual study involving little analysis or interpretation is generally divided into subtopics. (p. 482)

F _____ 23.   Informational reports are subdivided according to hypotheses or according to relative merits. (p. 482)

F _____ 24.   A primary concern when preparing informational reports is the readers' emotional reaction to the content. (p. 482)

T _____ 25.   Many informational reports are prepared on preprinted forms. (p. 482)

F _____ 26.   Analytical reports are primarily intended to educate readers. (p. 483)

F _____ 27.   The indirect approach is always used for analytical reports. (pp. 483–484)

T _____ 28.   Using the direct approach when your readers have reservations about your material may intensify their resistance to it. (p. 484)

T _____ 29.   A good organization for a justification report would be one built around recommendations. (p. 485)

T _____ 30.   Focusing on conclusions or recommendations is the most forceful and efficient way to organize an analytical report. (p. 487)

F _____ 31.   The main organizational plans used to convince skeptical readers to accept your conclusions and recommendations are the chronological, the sequential, and the spatial. (p. 488)

F _____ 32.   Although it is persuasive, the 2 + 2 = 4 approach is not an efficient way to organize an analytical report. (p. 489)

T _____ 33.   Reports based on the scientific method begin with a statement of the problem and a brief description of the hypothetical solution. (pp. 489–490)

T _____ 34.   One way to reduce the confusion presented by having too many alternatives is to establish a yardstick for evaluating all of them. (p. 493)

T _____ 35.   Using *I* and *you* gives a report a more informal tone. (p. 495)

F _____ 36.   To guarantee the objectivity of your report, be sure to use a formal style of writing. (p. 496)

T _____ 37.   Most organizations expect business reports to be written in an unobtrusive, impersonal style. (p. 496)

T _____ 38.   The opening provides readers with clues to the structure of a report. (p. 497)

T _____ 39.   If one main heading in a report is a noun phrase, all such headings should be noun phrases. (p. 498)

F _____ 40.   Generous use of transitions in a report will make up for otherwise poor organization. (p. 500)

MULTIPLE CHOICE

c _____ 1.   The first step in the report-writing process is to (p. 470)
   a. develop an outline.
   b. prepare a work plan.
   c. define the problem.
   d. conduct research.

d _____ 2.   When you factor a problem, you (p. 471)
   a. develop a schedule for your research.
   b. limit the scope of your investigation.
   c. develop alternative hypotheses.
   d. break the problem into a series of questions.

b _____ 3.   Which of the following is the *least* clear statement of purpose? (pp. 472–473)
   a. The purpose of this report is to determine which of four alternative investments will have the highest return."
   b. The purpose of this report is to analyze various investments."
   c. This report answers the question, 'Which of four investments will provide the highest return?'"
   d. This report will evaluate the return on four investments."

d _____ 4.   When drawing conclusions for a report, you (p. 475)
   a. make sure to take into account any information you know about that hasn't been included in the report.
   b. don't compromise with others working as a part of your team.
   c. suggest actions for the company to take based on the facts you have collected.
   d. interpret what the facts you have gathered mean.

a _____ 5. Conclusions differ from recommendations in that conclusions (p. 477)
a. are opinions or interpretations.
b. are objective.
c. are acceptable to readers.
d. suggest what ought to be done about the facts.

d _____ 6. The recommendations made in a report should be (p. 477)
a. the same as the conclusions.
b. opinions or interpretations.
c. what the audience wants to hear.
d. practical and offer real advantages to the organization.

a _____ 7. Conclusions and recommendations are stated at the beginning of a report (p. 479)
a. if readers are likely to agree with them.
b. if the indirect format is being used.
c. if the report is analytical.
d. never.

d _____ 8. You use the direct order for your report when (pp. 479–480)
a. you are the junior member in a status-conscious organization and you want to impress your superiors.
b. the material you are presenting is controversial.
c. your audience will be skeptical of your conclusions and recommendations.
d. you want to sound forceful, confident, and sure of yourself.

d _____ 9. When choosing between direct and indirect order, keep in mind that (p. 480)
a. you never combine the two approaches.
b. the longer the message, the more effective an indirect approach is likely to be.
c. the indirect approach saves time and makes the report easier to understand.
d. the order in real business reports is often difficult to classify.

b _____ 10. When you have leeway about the length and format of your report, you base your decisions on (p. 480)
a. previous personal experience.
b. your readers' needs.
c. company policy.
d. the nature of the subject matter.

c _____ 11. An external report of five pages or less (p. 481)
a. is usually written in memo format.
b. is usually done on a preprinted form.
c. can be in letter format.
d. is usually in manuscript format.

b _____ 12. A report will need to be longer if (p. 481)
a. the information is routine.
b. the material is controversial.
c. you are on familiar terms with the audience.
d. the audience is likely to agree with you.

b _____ 13. A study of a process would best be structured (p. 482)
   a. in order of importance.
   b. sequentially.
   c. spatially.
   d. categorically.

a _____ 14. Your main concern in informational reports is (p. 482)
   a. reader comprehension.
   b. audience persuasion.
   c. organization.
   d. reader-specified outlines.

c _____ 15. Which of the following is *not* a common type of organization for informational reports? (p. 482)
   a. According to importance
   b. According to chronology
   c. According to logic
   d. According to spatial orientation

a _____ 16. If you were writing a report reviewing five product lines, which method or organization would be most useful? (p. 482)
   a. According to importance
   b. According to chronology
   c. According to logic
   d. According to spatial orientation

c _____ 17. A drawback of the direct approach is that it may (p. 484)
   a. take longer than the indirect approach.
   b. be ineffective with complex or technical material.
   c. intensify the resistance of an audience that already has reservations about you or your material.
   d. require more judgment than the indirect approach.

d _____ 18. When organizing a report around recommendations, you (p. 485)
   a. establish the need for action in the introduction.
   b. introduce the benefit that can be achieved.
   c. list the steps (recommendations) required to achieve the benefit.
   d. do all of the above.

b _____ 19. Which of the following is *not* a common type of organization for analytical reports? (p. 488)
   a. The 2+2 approach
   b. The chronological approach
   c. The scientific approach
   d. The yardstick method

b _____ 20. In the 2 + 2 = 4 approach, the main points in your outline are (p. 488)
    a. quantitative in nature.
    b. the main reasons behind your conclusions.
    c. less important than your recommendations.
    d. more important than your recommendations.

c _____ 21. When writing analytical reports for skeptical readers, the most persuasive and efficient structure is (p. 488)
    a. the spatial approach.
    b. the sequential approach.
    c. the 2 + 2 = 4 approach.
    d. none of the above.

a _____ 22. A variation of the pattern associated with the scientific method is often useful for proposals because (pp. 489–490)
    a. you can suggest one or several solutions that you plan to investigate during the study.
    b. clients are more impressed by the scientific method than by other structures.
    c. it shortens the main section of the proposal.
    d. it is more persuasive than any other approach.

d _____ 23. The main drawback to the scientific method is that (p. 493)
    a. it presumes a sophisticated audience.
    b. it requires the use of manuscript format.
    c. it can be used only when the problem is a highly technical one.
    d. it requires that you discuss all the alternatives, even irrelevant or unproductive ones.

a _____ 24. The yardstick approach (p. 493)
    a. evaluates several alternatives against a set of criteria.
    b. is the opposite of the scientific method.
    c. is best used in informational reports.
    d. all of the above.

b _____ 25. A disadvantage of the yardstick approach is that (p. 493)
    a. it's not very logical.
    b. it can lead to a lot of repetition, which becomes boring in the report.
    c. it's not very useful for proposals.
    d. all of the above.

c _____ 26. The writing style for a report should be more formal if (p. 495)
    a. you know your readers reasonably well.
    b. your report is internal.
    c. the subject is controversial or complex.
    d. the report is relatively short.

b _____ 27. When it comes to time perspective in your report (p. 496)
    a. you should feel free to shift back and forth between the past and present tenses.
    b. you should be careful to observe the chronological sequence of events.
    c. you should make sure that none of your material is dated.
    d. you should keep everything in the past tense.

a _____ 28. The most important objective to achieve in the beginning of a report is to (p. 497)
  a. provide readers with a preview of the report's structure.
  b. grab the readers' attention.
  c. present your credentials.
  d. present conclusions and recommendations.

d _____ 29. When devising headings for sections of a report, keep in mind that (p. 498)
  a. you use as few as possible.
  b. descriptive headings are always preferable to informative headings.
  c. you never use such dull headings as "Conclusions" or "Recommendations."
  d. all same-level headings within a particular section are grammatically parallel.

a _____ 30. Transitional words and phrases (p. 500)
  a. tie ideas together and keep readers moving along the right track.
  b. help overcome poor organization.
  c. are essential to analytical reports but unnecessary in informational reports.
  d. do all of the above.

FILL-INS

1. The first step in planning a long report is to define the _____. (p. 470)

2. Breaking down a problem into a series of specific questions is called _____. (p. 471)

3. The statement of _____ defines the objective of the report. (p. 472)

4. Once you have defined the problem and outlined the issues for analysis, you need to prepare a _____ _____. (p. 473)

5. A _____ is a logical interpretation of the facts in your report. (p. 475)

6. A _____ suggests what ought to be done about the facts. (p. 477)

7. An _____ report is easy to organize because it provides nothing but facts. (p. 482)

8. Informational reports use a _____ organization. (p. 482)

9. In the _____ _____, reports are based on the accumulation of facts and figures developed around a list of reasons that add up to the main point. (p. 498)

10. Reports based on the _____ _____ begin with a statement of the problem and a brief description of the hypothetical solution. (p. 489)

11.   Using the _____ _____ is generally a useful way to reduce the confusion presented by having a lot of alternatives. (p. 493)

12.   If you know your readers reasonably well and if your report is likely to meet with their approval, you can generally adopt a less _____ tone. (p. 495)

13.   All same-level headings in a section of a report are in _____ form. (p. 498)

14.   Smooth _____ are useful tools for keeping readers on track as they read your report. (p. 500)

ANSWERS

1.   problem
2.   factoring
3.   purpose
4.   work plan
5.   conclusion
6.   recommendation
7.   informational

8.   topical
9.   2 + 2 = 4 approach
10.   scientific method
11.   yardstick approach
12.   formal
13.   parallel
14.   transitions

CHAPTER 15
COMPLETING FORMAL REPORTS AND PROPOSALS

TRUE OR FALSE

F _____ 1. If you use a personal computer, you can expect report writing to be a lot easier because people have very low expectations regarding computer-generated reports. (p. 512)

T _____ 2. Even when you use computers to generate your reports, you need to allow extra time for formatting and production. (p. 513)

T _____ 3. No matter how well you write a report, you won't always get the response you want and in fact may get no response at all. (p. 513)

T _____ 4. The longer a report, the greater number of components it usually contains. (p. 513)

F _____ 5. What distinguishes formal from informal reports is the more personal tone of formal reports. (p. 513)

F _____ 6. Because they fall at the beginning of a report, the prefatory parts are usually written first. (p. 514)

F _____ 7. Covers for reports are usually blank sheets of card stock that serve to protect that contents. (p. 514)

F _____ 8. A report title always starts with "A Study of" or "A Report on." (p. 514)

T _____ 9. It is sometimes acceptable for the title page to serve as the report cover. (p. 514)

T _____ 10. The letter of acceptance is the reply to the letter of authorization. (p. 515)

T _____ 11. The letter of transmittal says what you would say if you were handing the report directly to someone. (p. 515)

F _____ 12. The letter of transmittal should use the indirect approach, especially if the report is an analytical one. (p. 515)

T _____ 13. If a report does not have a synopsis, the letter of transmittal can be used to summarize the major findings, conclusions, and recommendations. (p. 515)

F _____ 14. The table of contents should always include all levels of headings for the report. (p. 515)

F _____ 15. A synopsis of a 15-page report is at least two pages long. (p. 516)

F _____ 16.   For a skeptical or hostile audience, you use an informative synopsis instead of a descriptive one. (p. 516)

F _____ 17.   A synopsis is generally more comprehensive than an executive summary. (pp. 517–518)

T _____ 18.   Unlike a synopsis, an executive summary may contain headings and visual aids. (p. 517)

T _____ 19.   Many reports, especially short ones, do not require a synopsis or executive summary. (p. 517)

F _____ 20.   Headings in formal reports are useful for the writer but not for the reader. (p. 517)

F _____ 21.   The main purpose of including visual aids in a report is to break up the monotony. (p. 517)

F _____ 22.   An introduction is never longer than a paragraph or two. (p. 517)

T _____ 23.   The introduction is a good place to include definitions of terms used in a report. (p. 518)

T _____ 24.   Any factors affecting the quality of a report, such as budget or time restrictions, are mentioned in the introduction. (p. 518)

F _____ 25.   Reports do not need an introduction if they have a synopsis and a letter of transmittal. (p. 519)

F _____ 26.   The "Summary" of a report is another name for the report's conclusions. (p. 519)

T _____ 27.   In reports that are intended to lead to action, the recommendations section is particularly important because it spells out exactly what should happen next. (p. 519)

F _____ 28.   It's best to make your source notes as conspicuous as possible, to give credibility to your report. (p. 520)

F _____ 29.   The most common items to include in an appendix are the bibliography and the index. (pp. 520–521)

F _____ 30.   Most organizations specify that all visual aids be placed in an appendix. (p. 521)

F _____ 31.   An index is a standard part of all long reports, whether published or not. (p. 521)

T _____ 32.   Bids to perform work under a contract and pleas for financial support from outsiders are nearly always formal. (p. 521)

F _____ 33.   The prefatory parts of a formal proposal are entirely different from the prefatory parts of other formal reports. (p. 522)

T _____ 34.   If a proposal is unsolicited, the letter of transmittal should follow the format for persuasive messages. (p. 522)

T _____ 35.   A synopsis or executive summary is less useful in a formal proposal than in other types of formal reports. (p. 522)

F _____ 36.   The organization of an unsolicited proposal is governed solely by the RFP. (p. 522)

F _____ 37.   The subheading "Overview of approach" is unlikely to appear anywhere in a formal proposal. (p. 523)

T _____ 38.   If your proposal is accepted, the work plan section becomes legally binding. (p. 523)

F _____ 39.   You are more likely to win a contract if you avoid outlining specific costs and just submit an overall price. (p. 524)

T _____ 40.   The summary or conclusion of a formal proposal is relatively brief, assertive, and confident. (p. 524)

MULTIPLE CHOICE

b _____ 1.   The traditional approach to producing business reports involves (p. 512)
   a.   subcontracting the work to a business writing firm.
   b.   working with colleagues within the organization.
   c.   working alone on a report from start to finish.
   d.   none of the above.

d _____ 2.   A formal report (p. 513)
   a.   must be at least 10 pages long.
   b.   is always for outsiders; internal reports are always informal.
   c.   is informational as opposed to analytical.
   d.   has a professional appearance and an impersonal tone.

c _____ 3.   Which of the following is *not* included in the prefatory parts of a formal report? (p. 514)
   a.   cover
   b.   letter of authorization
   c.   introduction
   d.   table of contents

c _____ 4.   What would be the best title for a formal report on the pros and cons of your company's acquisition of Freedman's Nuts & Bolts? (p. 514)
   a.   "To Acquire or Not to Acquire"
   b.   "A Study of the Feasibility of Angstrom Hardware Inc. Acquiring the Concern Currently Operating as Freedman's Nuts & Bolts"
   c.   "The Pros and Cons of Acquiring Freedman's Nuts & Bolts"
   d.   "Why Angstrom Should Forget About Acquiring Freedman"

b _____ 5.   The purpose of the title fly is to (p. 514)
a.   give the name of the company for which the report has been prepared.
b.   add a touch of formality to the report.
c.   protect the report from dirt and careless handling.
d.   provide a page for the reader to make notes on.

a _____ 6.   In addition to the title and submission date, the title page of a formal report should include information on (p. 514)
a.   the authorizer and the preparer.
b.   the authorizer and the recipient.
c.   the contents.
d.   the copyright.

a _____ 7.   The letter of transmittal (p. 515)
a.   should follow the good-news plan.
b.   has a more formal style than the report itself.
c.   is usually included as an appendix.
d.   all of the above.

b _____ 8.   The table of contents for a complex formal report lists (p. 515)
a.   every level of heading in the report plus all illustration and table titles.
b.   only the top two or three levels of headings plus prefatory and supplementary parts.
c.   everything but prefatory parts.
d.   everything but supplementary parts.

a _____ 9.   The synopsis section of a formal report (p. 516)
a.   is a concise overview of the report's most important points.
b.   is a short summary containing subheadings and visual aids.
c.   is usually anywhere from two to five pages.
d.   is all of the above.

b _____ 10.   An executive summary (p. 516)
a.   is never longer than a few paragraphs.
b.   may contain headings and visual aids.
c.   comes before the synopsis in the prefatory section of a report.
d.   is always included with reports longer than ten pages.

c _____ 11.   The headings in a report are (p. 517)
a.   unobtrusive.
b.   catchy and enigmatic to keep the readers' interest.
c.   useful tools for understanding the text.
d.   all of the above.

d _____ 12.   Which of the following is *not* usually included in the introduction to a report? (p. 518)
a.   A description of the sources and methods used
b.   An overview of the report's organization
c.   Definitions of terms used in the report
d.   Source documentation

b _____ 13. The best way to decide what to include in an introduction is to (p. 519)
a.   consult with more experienced report writers.
b.   figure out what kinds of information will most help your readers understand and accept the report.
c.   put in as many standard topics as you can cover in 10 pages or less.
d.   do a quick survey of potential readers.

b _____ 14. The detailed information necessary to support your conclusions and recommendations should be placed in (p. 519)
a.   the prefatory parts of a report.
b.   the body of a report.
c.   the appendix of a report.
d.   the supplementary parts of a report.

a _____ 15. The key findings of a report are stated in the (p. 519)
a.   summary.
b.   conclusions.
c.   recommendations.
d.   notes.

c _____ 16. Which of the following statements is a conclusion? (pp. 519–520)
a.   "Because the market for airplane parts is declining, Allied Industries should sell off its Turbo-Prop Inc. holdings by August 1990."
b.   "The number of commercial airliners manufactured has declined 75 percent since 1982; the production of private planes has decreased 86 percent during the same period."
c.   "The significant decline in production of both commercial and private aircraft in the 1980s and indications that this trend has continued into the 1990s do not bode well for investment in general aviation and its allied services."
d.   "After reviewing all the data on current trends in general aviation, I believe that Allied Industries should (1) hire a consultant more versed in the intricacies of this complex business, and (2) have the consultant make recommendations concerning the consolidation of our various general aviation holdings."

c _____ 17. The recommendations in an action-oriented report (p. 520)
a.   consist of the report's key findings.
b.   are the writer's analysis of what the findings mean.
c.   spell out exactly what should happen next.
d.   are the answers to the questions that led to the report.

b _____ 18. When making recommendations, it's important to (p. 520)
a.   address needed tasks in the most general terms possible.
b.   provide a schedule and specific task assignments.
c.   leave scheduling and specific task assignments for your supervisor to decide.
d.   play down the need for any action from your audience.

b _____ 19.   A short formal report would probably not include (p. 520)
  a. prefatory parts.
  b. supplementary parts.
  c. an index.
  d. a title page.

c _____ 20.   Materials in an appendix aren't incorporated into the text because (pp. 520—521)
  a. they are controversial.
  b. they include bad news.
  c. they are not directly relevant.
  d. they are boring.

a _____ 21.   The difference between formal proposals and other formal reports lies mainly in (p. 521)
  a. the text.
  b. the introduction.
  c. the prefatory parts.
  d. the appendixes.

b _____ 22.   The prefatory parts of a formal proposal may include (p. 522)
  a. a letter of authorization.
  b. a copy of the RFP.
  c. an index.
  d. visual aids.

a _____ 23.   Transmittal letters for unsolicited proposals should follow the form for (p. 522)
  a. persuasive messages.
  b. bad-news messages.
  c. good-news messages.
  d. routine messages.

d _____ 24.   In a formal proposal, a synopsis or executive summary may be (p. 522)
  a. essential for highlighting your competitive advantage.
  b. useful if the proposal is fairly short.
  c. placed in an appendix.
  d. unnecessary.

b _____ 25.   The organization of a solicited proposal is governed by (p. 522)
  a. the topic of the proposal.
  b. the RFP.
  c. company policy.
  d. the writer's preference.

c _____ 26.   A typical subheading in the introduction of a formal proposal would be (p. 523)
  a. "Visual Aids"
  b. "Cost Analysis"
  c. "Scope"
  d. "Qualifications"

c _____ 27. In a formal proposal, the statement of qualifications is frequently (p. 523)
     a. unnecessary.
     b. optional.
     c. an important selling point.
     d. none of the above.

d _____ 28. In the costs section of a formal proposal, you (pp. 523–524)
     a. provide rough estimates of the overall cost of the project.
     b. bid low to increase the chances that the client will accept your proposal.
     c. bid high so that the client will realize that you do high-quality work.
     d. provide a detailed breakdown of the estimated costs.

a _____ 29. In a formal proposal, it pays to be (p. 524)
     a. as thorough and accurate as possible.
     b. as brief as possible.
     c. as technical as possible.
     d. as slick as possible.

d _____ 30. The summary portion of a formal proposal provides an opportunity to (p. 524)
     a. summarize the merits of your approach.
     b. re-emphasize the skills and experience you bring to the project.
     c. stress the benefits of choosing your company to do the project.
     d. do all of the above.

FILL-INS

1. The cover, title page, and table of contents are among the _____ parts of a formal report. (p. 514)

2. The _____ _____ is a plain sheet of paper with only the title of the report on it. (p. 514)

3. A letter of _____ is a written acknowledgment of the letter of authorization. (p. 515)

4. The letter of _____ conveys the report to the readers. (p. 515)

5. A(n) _____ synopsis presents the main points of a report in the order in which they appear in the text. (p. 516)

6. A(n) _____ synopsis simply tells what the report is about. (p. 516)

7. An _____ _____ is a fully developed "mini" version of the report itself. (p. 516)

8.   A writer's analysis of what the findings of a report mean would typically be placed in a section labeled
      _____. (p. 519)

9.   The appendix, bibliography, and index make up the _____ parts of a formal report.
      (p. 520)

10.   An _____ contains materials that are too lengthy or too bulky to include in the main
      body of a report. (p. 520)

11.   A _____ is a list of sources consulted when preparing a report. (p. 521)

12.   Instead of a letter of authorization, a proposal contains a _____
      _____ _____ issued by the client. (p. 522)

13.   If your proposal is accepted, the _____ _____ will become
      contractually binding. (p. 523)

14.   A _____ section is your last opportunity to convince the reader to accept your
      proposal. (p. 524)

ANSWERS

1. prefatory
2. title fly
3. acceptance
4. transmittal
5. informative
6. descriptive
7. executive summary

8.   conclusions
9.   supplementary
10. appendix
11. bibliography
12. request for proposal
13. work plan
14. summary (conclusion)

CHAPTER 16
GIVING SPEECHES AND ORAL PRESENTATIONS

TRUE OR FALSE

F _____ 1. If your speech doesn't capture the interest of your audience immediately, you can always regain their interest at a later point. (p. 562)

F _____ 2. It's not as important to research your audience for an oral presentation as it is for a written one. (p. 563)

T _____ 3. Planning an oral message is similar to planning a written message. (p. 564)

T _____ 4. The main idea for a speech clarifies how the audience can benefit from the speaker's message. (p. 564)

T _____ 5. Developing the main idea of a presentation by using a "you" attitude helps keep the audience's attention. (p. 564)

F _____ 6. All speeches and presentations are organized the same way you would organize letters or memos. (p. 565)

F _____ 7. If your purpose is to analyze, persuade, or collaborate, organize your material chronologically. (p. 565)

F _____ 8. Simplicity of organization is important only if your speech is long. (p. 567)

F _____ 9. If you plan to use your outline as the "script" for your speech, you stick to one- or two-word topic headings. (p. 568)

T _____ 10. Your outline is a good place to include annotations about the tone or body language you want to use. (p. 568)

F _____ 11. The speech outline is not an appropriate place to include notes about the visual aids. (p. 568)

F _____ 12. If you are delivering a one-hour speech, you allow 15 minutes for the introduction, 30 minutes for the body, and 15 minutes for the conclusion. (p. 569)

T _____ 13. If your audience is skeptical, you should plan on a longer speech or presentation. (p. 569)

T _____ 14. In general, you use a casual style when speaking to small groups and a formal style for large groups. (p. 569)

T _____ 15. A major difference between preparing a speech and preparing a formal report is that a speech requires you to adjust your technique to the oral mode. (p. 569)

F _____ 16.   When you speak in front of a group, you are transmitting information, not receiving it. (p. 570)

T _____ 17.   As a speaker, the more you interact with the audience, the less control you have. (p. 570)

F _____ 18.   If you are addressing a group of business executives about a serious matter, it's best to break the ice by telling a joke or a personal anecdote. (p. 571)

T _____ 19.   You must establish credibility with your audience if you want them to accept your message. (p. 571)

T _____ 20.   Having someone else introduce you can help establish your credibility as a speaker. (p. 571)

F _____ 21.   Giving your audience a preview of what you'll be talking about will reduce their interest and attention. (p. 571)

F _____ 22.   Transitional words and sentences are less important in oral presentations than in written reports. (p. 572–573)

T _____ 23.   To keep an audience's attention, try to present every point in light of the audience's needs and values. (p. 573)

F _____ 24.   The ending is the least important part of a speech. (p. 573)

T _____ 25.   It's best to devote about 10 percent of your speech to the conclusion. (p. 573)

F _____ 26.   When concluding a speech, don't bore your audience by restating points you already made in the body of the speech. (p. 573)

T _____ 27.   If the action you advocate in a speech is likely to be difficult, use the final summary to point up pitfalls and alert people to possible difficulties. (p. 574)

T _____ 28.   Even if parts of your speech have been downbeat, you always try to close on a positive note. (p. 575)

F _____ 29.   To make your speech memorable, you plan for a dramatic finale. (p. 575)

F _____ 30.   You include a question-and-answer session after a speech only if you have not filled the allotted time. (p. 575)

F _____ 31.   The best way to prepare for a speech is to memorize the whole thing. (p. 576)

T _____ 32.   Making a speech with the help of an outline or note cards is the most effective and easiest delivery mode. (p. 672)

F _____ 33.   It is considered rude to ask to see the facilities where you will be giving a speech prior to the presentation. (p. 576)

T _____ 34. To help overcome stage fright, concentrate on your message and your audience, not on yourself. (p. 578)

F _____ 35. You can help keep your composure during a speech by gripping the lectern with both hands. (p. 579)

F _____ 36. Graphic visual aids used in oral presentations are enlarged but otherwise identical to the visual aids that appear in a report. (p. 579)

F _____ 37. If you use a pointer in your presentation, you should keep it in your hands at all times as a visual "prop." (p. 579)

T _____ 38. If you must dim the light to show slides, be sure to stand in a lighted area and face the audience while describing the material on the slides. (p. 580)

T _____ 39. It's often a good idea to save some of your dramatic statistics to use as ammunition during the question-and-answer session following your speech. (p. 580)

T _____ 40. If you encounter hostility during a question-and-answer session following a speech, avoid arguing and try not to show your feelings. (p. 580)

MULTIPLE CHOICE

a _____ 1. Speeches and oral presentations are much like any other messages in that (p. 562)
   a. they require similar preparation.
   b. the size of the groups to which they are delivered is similar.
   c. the interaction between the audience and speaker is similar.
   d. they deal with emotional or personal issues to a similar extent.

b _____ 2. When you prepare a speech or presentation, your first step involves (p. 562)
   a. defining your purpose.
   b. analyzing your audience.
   c. planning the content, length, and style of your speech or presentation.
   d. all of the above.

c _____ 3. The four basic purposes of speeches and oral presentations are to (p. 562)
   a. analyze, categorize, summarize, and synthesize.
   b. regulate, modulate, translate, and validate.
   c. inform, persuade, motivate, and entertain.
   d. respond, explain, revise, and illustrate.

a _____ 4. Analyzing your audience helps you (p. 563)
   a. gear the style and content of your speech to audience needs and interests.
   b. remember to keep your speech or oral presentation short.
   c. define your purpose.
   d. prepare a detailed, informative outline.

b _____ 5.   When planning a speech or presentation, your first step is to (p. 564)
     a.   develop an outline.
     b.   define the main idea.
     c.   write the introduction.
     d.   decide on the delivery style.

c _____ 6.   When organizing a speech, use the indirect order if your purpose is to (p. 564)
     a.   entertain and the audience is resistant.
     b.   motivate and the audience is receptive.
     c.   persuade and the audience is resistant.
     d.   inform and the audience is receptive.

a _____ 7.   Longer speeches and presentations are organized like (p. 565)
     a.   reports.
     b.   memos.
     c.   letters.
     d.   e-mail messages.

a _____ 8.   When preparing an outline for your speech, keep in mind that (p. 568)
     a.   it can serve as your final "script."
     b.   you should keep each item to two- to three-word descriptions of what you will say.
     c.   you can leave out all transitions.
     d.   this is not the place to include "stage directions."

d _____ 9.   The average speaker talks at a rate of about (p. 569)
     a.   50 words a minute.
     b.   ten double-spaced pages an hour.
     c.   2,000 words an hour.
     d.   one paragraph per minute.

a _____ 10.   To reduce the formality of a talk (p. 569)
     a.   deliver your remarks in a conversational tone.
     b.   use a large room.
     c.   seat the audience in rows.
     d.   do all of the above.

c _____ 11.   Formal speeches differ from formal reports in that (p. 570)
     a.   the indirect approach is never used.
     b.   organization is not as important.
     c.   loss of control is always a possibility.
     d.   visual aids are less important.

d _____ 12.   To arouse interest at the start of a speech, whether it's serious or light, (pp. 570–571)
     a.   always start things off with a joke.
     b.   do something dramatic.
     c.   tease the audience by not mentioning specifically what you'll be talking about.
     d.   do none of the above.

b _____ 13.   In the introduction to your speech (p. 571)
      a.   discuss the three or four main points on your outline.
      b.   establish credibility.
      c.   ask for audience input.
      d.   boast about your qualifications.

c _____ 14.   As a speaker, your credibility depends on (p. 571)
      a.   having outstanding credentials.
      b.   arousing interest in the audience.
      c.   quickly establishing a good relationship with the audience.
      d.   the points you make in the main body of your speech.

b _____ 15.   "Now that we've reviewed the problem, let's take a look at some solutions" is an example of (p. 573)
      a.   a poor transition.
      b.   a good transition between major sections of a speech.
      c.   a small link between sentences or paragraphs in a speech.
      d.   the kind of wording that should never appear in a speech.

c _____ 16.   To hold your audience's attention during the body of your speech, (p. 573)
      a.   make at least seven or eight main points.
      b.   include numerous abstract ideas.
      c.   relate your subject to your audience's needs.
      d.   do all of the above.

b _____ 17.   What percentage of the total presentation time should be devoted to the ending? (p. 573)
      a.   1 percent
      b.   10 percent
      c.   20 percent
      d.   30 percent

a _____ 18.   When you have covered all the main points in your speech, (pp. 573–574)
      a.   reinforce your theme by repeating and summarizing the three or four main supporting points.
      b.   wrap up as quickly as possible.
      c.   avoid using such phrases as "To sum it all up" and "In conclusion."
      d.   do all of the above.

c _____ 19.   If your speech or presentation requires the audience to reach a decision or take some specific action, (p. 574)
      a.   go directly to the question-and-answer session after you cover the main points of your speech.
      b.   close your speech on a note of uncertainty.
      c.   close your speech by explaining who is responsible for doing what.
      d.   lead people to believe that the decision will be easy to carry out.

a _____ 20. You always close your speech (p. 575)
   a. on a positive note.
   b. by leaving the audience with a feeling of incompleteness, which you can resolve in the question-and-answer period.
   c. with something dramatic or flamboyant.
   d. by introducing some new ideas for the audience to think about.

b _____ 21. You defer questions from the audience until the end of your speech when (p. 575)
   a. the audience is small.
   b. the audience is hostile.
   c. the purpose of the speech is to persuade or to collaborate.
   d. your topic is boring.

c _____ 22. A question-and-answer period after a speech (pp. 575–576)
   a. is usually unnecessary.
   b. is helpful only if the purpose of the speech is to motivate or entertain.
   c. is one of the most important parts of any presentation.
   d. is included only for small audiences.

c _____ 23. Probably the most effective and easiest mode of speech delivery is (p. 576)
   a. memorization.
   b. reading from a prepared script.
   c. speaking from notes.
   d. impromptu speaking.

b _____ 24. You might be better off reading your presentation if (p. 576)
   a. you have only a short time in which to deliver your message.
   b. your message is technical or complex.
   c. it is an impromptu talk.
   d. you have a pleasant-sounding voice.

c _____ 25. An unrehearsed speech is delivered (p. 576)
   a. only in informal situations.
   b. in order to test the speaker.
   c. impromptu.
   d. with the help of an outline.

b _____ 26. Which of the following is *not* a good way to deal with stage fright? (pp. 577–578)
   a. Prepare more material than necessary.
   b. Concentrate on your nervousness.
   c. Take a few deep breaths before speaking.
   d. Have your first sentence memorized and on the tip of your tongue.

c _____ 27. If you have access to a laser pointer (p. 579)
   a. you should avoid using it.
   b. you should keep it in your hands throughout your presentation.
   c. you should use it judiciously.
   d. you should have fun with it by pointing it at various people in the audience.

b _____ 28. When you need to dim the lights for a slide presentation (p. 580)
     a. stand in the shadows so the audience can attend to the screen.
     b. keep your back to the audience so you can look at the screen yourself.
     c. once you've finished with a slide, remove it and try not to go to the next slide right away.
     d. all of the above.

d _____ 29. If you don't have enough time to answer a question fully, it is best to (p. 580)
     a. refer the questioner to another source.
     b. give what information you can before your time runs out.
     c. say, "Sorry, but we just don't have time for that now."
     d. offer to get together after the presentation to discuss the issue.

c _____ 30. When your allotted time is up, prepare your audience for the end by (p. 581)
     a. beginning to pack your materials.
     b. refusing to acknowledge those who wish to speak.
     c. saying that you will take one more question.
     d. waving good-bye and leaving the podium.

FILL-INS

1. Speeches and presentations can be categorized according to their _____, which may be to motivate, entertain, inform, analyze, persuade, or collaborate. (p. 562)

2. Before planning a speech, you analyze your _____. (p. 563)

3. The _____ _____ of a speech is a you-oriented statement that points up how the audience can benefit from your subject and purpose. (p. 564)

4. You can use your _____ as your final "script" for a speech. (p. 568)

5. For a large audience and an important event, your tone will be _____. (p. 569)

6. The _____ to your speech captures the audience's attention and inspires confidence. (p. 570)

7. At the beginning of a speech, you need to establish _____ with your audience. (p. 571)

8. Whatever the topic of your speech, you should always try to end on a _____ note. (p. 575)

9. In addition to having an introduction, a body, and a final summary, your speech should allow for a _____-_____-_____ session. (p. 575)

10. If you are asked to speak without any advance warning, your talk will be _____. (p. 576)

11. You can overcome _____ _____ by concentrating on your message and your audience, not on your anxiety. (p. 577)

12. During a speech, take particular care to maintain _____ _____ with your audience. (p. 579)

13. Using _____ _____ such as flip charts and slides can help you maintain and revive audience interest. (p. 579)

14. If you are using a _____ _____ that puts a dot of light on the desired part of your visual, don't overdo it. (p. 579)

ANSWERS

1. purpose
2. audience
3. main idea
4. outline (notes)
5. formal
6. introduction (opening)
7. credibility

8. positive
9. question-and-answer
10. impromptu
11. stage fright (anxiety)
12. eye contact
13. visual aids
14. laser pointer

CHAPTER 17
WRITING RÉSUMÉS AND APPLICATION LETTERS

TRUE OR FALSE

F _____ 1. Taking tests to identify your aptitudes, interests, and personality traits will reveal the "perfect" job for you. (p. 590)

F _____ 2. When you are just starting out, it is unproductive to set future salary and career advancement goals. (p. 591)

F _____ 3. Location is not a factor in your choice of jobs. What you do is more important than where you do it. (p. 591)

T _____ 4. When considering your ideal job, you should think about what kind of corporate culture you'd find most desirable. (p. 591)

F _____ 5. Knowing a foreign language or having studied abroad will have little effect on your employment chances. (p. 591)

T _____ 6. As part of your job search, it's a good idea to keep abreast of business and financial news. (p. 593)

F _____ 7. You can find information about job hunting on the Internet, but it's not a good source for information on specific job openings. (p. 594)

F _____ 8. Few organizations respond to unsolicited résumés. (p. 597)

T _____ 9. A résumé is a form of advertising designed to help you get an interview. (p. 597)

F _____ 10. The purpose of a résumé is to list all your skills and abilities. (p. 597)

T _____ 11. It's possible to include too much information in a résumé. (p. 597)

F _____ 12. If you need to make corrections on your résumé, write them in neatly by hand. (p. 598)

T _____ 13. As a rule, you try to limit your résumé to one page. (p. 598)

F _____ 14. To fit everything on one page, it's okay to sacrifice white space on your résumé. (p. 599)

F _____ 15. When giving your background and qualifications on a résumé, you always use complete sentences. (p. 599)

F _____ 16. The only proper heading for a résumé is "Résumé." (pp. 600)

F _____ 17.   If you plan to include a career objective or summary of qualifications in your résumé, you make it as vague as possible to keep from limiting your prospects. (p. 600)

T _____ 18.   If your immediate career objective differs from your ultimate one, you can include both in a single statement. (p. 600)

T _____ 19.   The education section of your résumé includes any relevant seminars or workshops you have attended. (p. 601)

T _____ 20.   If you have worked in your chosen field for a year or more, your résumé de-emphasizes your educational background. (p. 601)

F _____ 21.   In the work experience section of your résumé, you leave out any jobs that do not relate directly to your career objective. (p. 601)

F _____ 22.   Your résumé lists past jobs in chronological order, with the first job first and the current job last. (p. 601)

T _____ 23.   When listing work experience on a résumé, you emphasize significant accomplishments in each job. (p. 601)

T _____ 24.   A good résumé can be customized for different situations and different employers.   (p. 602)

F _____ 25.   It is inappropriate to mention community activities or volunteer work on a résumé. (p. 603)

F _____ 26.   All résumés should be organized chronologically. (p. 604)

T _____ 27.   A functional résumé is organized around a list of accomplishments and focuses on the person's areas of competence. (p. 604)

T _____ 28.   To make your résumé scannable, you need to convert it to ASCII format. (p. 608)

F _____ 29.   Some examples of key words to include in your electronic résumé would be "works hard," "knows foreign languages," and "gets along well with others." (p. 610)

T _____ 30.   It is preferable to submit your scannable résumé by e-mail rather than by fax or regular mail. (p. 611)

T _____ 31.   Prospective employers do not like résumés that are gimmicky, boastful, or too slick. (p. 612)

F _____ 32.   Unsolicited application letters are those sent in response to want ads for job openings. (p. 614)

T _____ 33.   An unsolicited job application letter may get more individual attention than a solicited one. (p. 614)

T _____ 34.   An application letter follows the format for a persuasive message. (p. 614)

T _____ 35. The opening paragraph of an unsolicited application letter needs to grab the reader's attention and interest. (p. 614)

F _____ 36. It is inappropriate to "drop names" of mutual acquaintances in an application letter. (p. 614)

T _____ 37. The opening of an application letter states one's reason for writing. (p. 615)

T _____ 38. In the middle part of an application letter, you spell out your "selling points" and other potential benefits to your employer. (pp. 616–617)

F _____ 39. You should always write for a job application form—never drop by the employer's office to pick one up. (p. 617)

F _____ 40. If your application letter and résumé fail to bring a response within a month or so, you can assume that the company is not interested and cross it off your list. (p. 620)

MULTIPLE CHOICE

c _____ 1. Before trying to identify employers who are likely to want you and vice versa, you begin by (p. 590)
   a. limiting your search to a particular industry or functional specialty.
   b. talking to friends who have interesting jobs.
   c. analyzing what you have to offer and what you hope to get from your job.
   d. reading carefully through company literature from a wide variety of firms.

b _____ 2. Which of the following is an example of corporate culture? (p. 591)
   a. modern office space
   b. a well-defined hierarchy
   c. computer-assisted customer relations
   d. profit-making status

b _____ 3. If you do not have actual job experience, you can increase your chances of being hired by (p. 591–592)
   a. making random phone calls to local businesses and asking them whether they are hiring.
   b. spending as much time as possible surfing the Internet.
   c. taking courses or workshops that will expand your knowledge and experience.
   d. all of the above.

a _____ 4. Organizations find new employees chiefly through (p. 594)
   a. employee referrals and personal contacts.
   b. help-wanted ads.
   c. employment agencies.
   d. on-campus interviews.

c _____ 5. The purpose of a résumé is to (p. 597)
    a. induce the reader to hire you.
    b. list all your skills and abilities.
    c. get you an interview.
    d. take the place of an application letter.

b _____ 6. To achieve the best physical appearance for your résumé, you (p. 599)
    a. have it prepared by a professional résumé service.
    b. leave ample margins all around.
    c. use colored paper.
    d. use a variety of typefaces in various colors.

c _____ 7. Your résumé emphasizes (pp. 598–599)
    a. your work experience.
    b. your education.
    c. your strongest, most impressive qualifications.
    d. your career objective.

d _____ 8. Which of the following would be the most desirable wording to use on a résumé?
    a. "I was in charge of a staff of six employees."
    b. "I supervised six employees."
    c. "Was in charge of entire departmental staff."
    d. "supervised staff of six employees."

b _____ 9. If you are still a student and have little work experience, your résumé should emphasize (p. 600)
    a. summer jobs you have held.
    b. your educational background.
    c. your hobbies and interests.
    d. volunteer work you've done and service organizations in which you've been active.

a _____ 10. When you describe your work experience on your résumé (p. 601)
    a. start with your most recent job and work back chronologically.
    b. describe one or two jobs in detail so that employers get an idea of your work ethic.
    c. list only full-time positions.
    d. try to come up with fancier titles for the jobs you've held.

c _____ 11. When listing activities and achievements, you should probably avoid mentioning (p. 604)
    a. participation in athletics.
    b. involvement in fund-raising or community service activities.
    c. membership in political or religious organizations.
    d. speaking, writing, or tutoring experience.

a _____ 12. In the "Personal Data" section of your résumé, you list (p. 604)
    a. hobbies or miscellaneous experiences that may help you get the job.
    b. any health problems or disabilities you have, whether or not they may affect your job performance.
    c. your age, marital status, race, color, religion, and national origin, which are required by law.
    d. any experience in the military, whether or not it has a bearing on the job.

c _____ 13. Do not include on your résumé items that could encourage discrimination, such as (p. 604)
   a. home address.
   b. hobbies.
   c. marital status.
   d. military service.

a _____ 14. The most traditional way to organize a résumé is (p. 604)
   a. chronologically.
   b. functionally.
   c. geographically.
   d. alphabetically.

a _____ 15. The best organization for the résumé of someone with a strong employment history along a progressive career path would be (p. 604)
   a. chronological.
   b. functional.
   c. targeted.
   d. portfolio.

b _____ 16. If you are planning a career change and want to prepare a résumé emphasizing skills that qualify you for a job in your new field, the best organizational plan for your résumé would be (pp. 604–605)
   a. chronological.
   b. functional.
   c. targeted.
   d. indirect.

c _____ 17. A type of résumé that emphasizes a candidate's skills and accomplishments while also including a complete job history is termed (p. 607)
   a. a chronological résumé.
   b. a functional résumé.
   c. a combination résumé.
   d. an indirect résumé.

b _____ 18. To prepare your résumé for the scanning process (p. 608)
   a. you need to rewrite the whole thing.
   b. you need to convert it to plain text (ASCII) format.
   c. you will need a special software program.
   d. all of the above.

a _____ 19. An electronic résumé differs from a standard print résumé in that (p. 610)
   a. it includes a list of key words.
   b. the Work Experience section always gets listed first.
   c. you leave out the Education section.
   d. all of the above.

c _____ 20.   The best way to send a scannable résumé is (p. 611)
   a.   through regular mail.
   b.   by fax.
   c.   via e-mail as part of the body of the e-mail message.
   d.   via e-mail as an attached file.

d _____ 21.   Which of the following is *not* a common problem that employers see in résumés? (pp. 611–612)
   a.   They are too slick.
   b.   They are amateurish.
   c.   They are filled with misspellings and grammatical errors.
   d.   They are too simple and concise.

b _____ 22.   You'll impress prospective employers with your application letter if you (p. 612)
   a.   use a gimmicky layout.
   b.   show that you know something about the organization.
   c.   use a personal, "chummy" tone.
   d.   do all of the above.

a _____ 23.   Sending an unsolicited application letter to an employer will probably (p. 614)
   a.   result in your application getting more attention than it might receive if it were in response to an advertised opening.
   b.   irritate the personnel office staff.
   c.   mean that your letter will not get read.
   d.   neither help nor harm your chances for an interview with the employer.

c _____ 24.   The main difference between solicited and unsolicited application letters is in (p. 614)
   a.   the length.
   b.   the way qualifications are presented.
   c.   the way the letter begins.
   d.   the way the letter closes.

d _____ 25.   Which of the following would be the most effective opening for an unsolicited application letter? (pp. 614–615)
   a.   "Hi! Let me introduce myself. My name is Clydene Desmond, and I'd like to apply for any positions you may have for graphic artists."
   b.   "I hear you've been looking for a graphic artist. Look no further."
   c.   "I've just graduated from the Pasadena School of Graphic Arts, and somebody gave me your name as a company that could use my services."
   d.   "As a recent honors graduate of one of the top graphic arts programs in the country, I could make a strong contribution to Westec's publications division."

a _____ 26.   A solicited letter written in response to a job advertisement begins (p. 615)
   a.   by identifying the publication in which the ad ran.
   b.   by identifying the writer of the letter.
   c.   with an attention-getting device.
   d.   with a request for a job application.

a _____ 27. In the middle section of a job application letter, you (p. 615)
  a. summarize your qualifications that are directly related to the job and provide specific evidence of job-related qualities.
  b. give your entire work history, in case the employer doesn't read your résumé.
  c. mention any ways in which you do not meet the job qualifications but point out that you are willing to learn.
  d. do all of the above.

c _____ 28. In the closing paragraph of your application letter, you (pp. 616–617)
  a. thank the reader for taking the time to read your résumé.
  b. apologize for your lack of experience.
  c. ask for an interview and make the interview easy to arrange.
  d. introduce the subject of salary.

a _____ 29. When filling out a job application form, you (pp. 617–618)
  a. are as thorough and accurate as possible.
  b. write additional information about yourself on the back if the form doesn't ask the right questions.
  c. indicate the exact salary you want.
  d. do all of the above.

b _____ 30. If your application letter and résumé fail to bring a response within a month or so, you (p. 620)
  a. call to find out why you haven't heard from the prospective employer.
  b. write a follow-up letter.
  c. cross this particular job possibility off your list.
  d. send another copy of your application letter and résumé.

FILL-INS

1. A _____ is a form of self-advertisement designed to get you an interview. (p. 597)

2. For a résumé, use short, crisp phrases starting with _____ verbs. (p. 599)

3. The _____ _____ section of a résumé states what you wish to accomplish in your work. (p. 600)

4. In the _____ section of your résumé you list schools you've attended and degrees you've received. (p. 600)

5. In the _____ _____ section of your résumé you list jobs you've had and responsibilities you've held on those jobs. (p. 601)

6.   Hobbies and military service information may be listed in the _____
_____ section of your résumé. (p. 604)

7.   The most traditional way to organize a résumé is _____. (p. 604)

8.   A _____ résumé is organized around a list of skills and accomplishments. (p. 604)

9.   To prepare an electronic résumé, you need to make its format appropriate for _____
into an electronic database. (p. 608)

10.   To change your traditional paper résumé into a scannable one, you must convert it to plain-text or
_____ format. (p. 608)

11.   An electronic résumé should include a list of _____ _____ that
will help employers identify your skills. (p. 608)

12.   To accompany your résumé, you can prepare an individualized _____ letter. (p. 612)

13.   A _____ application letter is sent in response to an announced opening, whereas an
_____ application letter is sent to an organization that has not announced an opening.
(pp. 612, 614)

14.   A job application letter follows the _____ organizational plan. (p. 407)

ANSWERS

1.	résumé	8.	functional
2.	action	9.	scanning
3.	career objective	10.	ASCII
4.	education	11.	key words
5.	work experience	12.	application
6.	personal data	13.	solicited, unsolicited
7.	chronologically	14.	AIDA

CHAPTER 18
INTERVIEWING FOR EMPLOYMENT AND FOLLOWING UP

TRUE OR FALSE

F _____ 1. Recruiting procedures are essentially the same for both large and small companies. (p. 628)

T _____ 2. Most employers interview an applicant two or three times before deciding whether to offer a person a job. (p. 629)

T _____ 3. Preliminary screening interviews tend to be structured, with each applicant being asked the same questions. (p. 630)

T _____ 4. According to experts, it takes an average of ten interviews to get one job offer. (p. 631)

F _____ 5. An open-ended interview tends to be formal and highly structured.. (p. 631)

T _____ 6. During a stress interview, you might be asked pointed questions designed to anger or unsettle you. (p. 631)

F _____ 7. You prepare for a video interview the same way you would prepare for an in-person interview. (p. 632)

F _____ 8. Employers try to avoid job applicants who have high EQs. (pp. 632–633)

T _____ 9. Some interviewers want to hear about a job applicant's hobbies and interests. (p. 633)

T _____ 10. More and more companies are requiring job applicants to take honesty tests. (p. 634)

T _____ 11. You can prepare for a job interview by anticipating the questions that will be asked and rehearsing answers to each one. (p. 637)

F _____ 12. Job applicants don't ask questions during an interview; they are there to answer questions, not to ask them. (p. 637)

F _____ 13. As you ask questions during a job interview, keep a notepad handy so that you can record the interviewer's answers exactly and make full notes about other information you want to remember. (p. 639)

F _____ 14. It's only natural to be self-conscious in interviews, since interviewers will be hyperaware of your weaknesses. (p. 639)

T _____ 15. Staging mock interviews can help you identify self-defeating nonverbal behaviors and speech mannerisms. (pp. 640-641)

T _____ 16.   Part of your preparation for job interviews is an evaluation of your voice tone and speaking habits. (p. 641)

T _____ 17.   The appropriate clothing for most job interviews is something conservative and businesslike, such as a dark blue suit. (p. 642)

F _____ 18.   Because a job interview is a serious situation, you try to smile as little as possible. (p. 642)

T _____ 19.   It's a good idea to take extra copies of your résumé with you to an interview, as well as a list of questions to ask and any past correspondence about the position. (p. 642)

F _____ 20.   Most interviewers expect applicants to be a few minutes late for their appointment. (p. 643)

T _____ 21.   During a screening interview, it's best to call attention to one key aspect of your background that will make you more memorable. (p. 643)

T _____ 22.   An important purpose of the final job interview is to determine whether there is a good psychological fit between you and the job. (p. 644)

F _____ 23.   Of the three stages of a job interview, the close is the most important. (p. 644)

T _____ 24.   Body language is particularly important during the warm-up phase of a job interview. (p. 644)

F _____ 25.   If you get off to a bad start in a job interview, you can usually turn things around with an impressive close. (p. 644)

F _____ 26.   During the question-and-answer phase of an interview, try to keep your answers short; usually just a yes or no will do. (p. 644)

T _____ 27.   It is illegal for an interviewer to ask about your religious affiliation, your marital status, or how many children you have. (p. 645)

F _____ 28.   If you are asked an unlawful question during a job interview, you should always refuse to answer. (p. 645)

F _____ 29.   At the close of an interview, you can impress the interviewer with your assertiveness by pressing for an immediate decision. (p. 646)

F _____ 30.   A job interviewer will expect you to be the one who raises the issue of salary. (p. 646)

F _____ 31.   Once an interviewer states the salary for a job offer, you never try to negotiate it. (p. 646)

T _____ 32.   You don't inquire about fringe benefits until you know you have a job offer. (p. 646)

T _____ 33.   Immediately after a job interview, it's a good idea to record the answers you received to your questions and an evaluation of your performance during the interview. (pp. 646–647)

F _____ 34. After an interview you should never follow up with a phone call—use regular mail or e-mail. (p. 648)

T _____ 35. Even if you feel that you have little chance for the job, you should still send a thank-you message. (p. 648)

T _____ 36. When inquiring about a hiring decision as a follow-up to a job interview, you use the general plan for a direct request. (pp. 649–650)

F _____ 37. It is risky to ask an employer for a time extension to consider a job offer because most employers want an immediate answer. (p. 650)

T _____ 38. A letter accepting a job is legally binding. (p. 651)

F _____ 39. When declining a job offer or resigning, your letter follows the direct plan. (p. 651)

F _____ 40. If you are unhappy in your current job, your letter of resignation is a good place to vent your negative feelings. (p. 651)

MULTIPLE CHOICE

c _____ 1. Employers use preliminary screening interviews to (p. 629)
   a. find out as much as possible about each job candidate.
   b. give employment tests.
   c. narrow the field of applicants.
   d. offer jobs to the best candidates.

b _____ 2. During a screening interview, your best approach is to (p. 630)
   a. ask as many questions as possible.
   b. follow the interviewer's lead.
   c. expand on your answers as much as possible so that the interviewer knows you are at ease.
   d. keep as low a profile as you can; this is not the time to try to differentiate yourself from other candidates.

d _____ 3. In the second round of interviews, your best approach is to (p. 630)
   a. stick to brief, yes and no answers to the interview questions.
   b. relate your training and experience to the organization's needs.
   c. inquire about salary and benefits.
   d. do all the above.

a _____ 4. An interview in which a job candidate is criticized or provoked is a type of (p. 631)
   a. stress interview.
   b. structured interview.
   c. screening interview.
   d. situational interview.

d _____ 5   An interview in which a job candidate is placed in a hands-on situation and asked to do job-related tasks is a type of (p. 632)
    a.   stress interview.
    b.   structured interview.
    c.   screening interview.
    d.   situational interview.

c _____ 6.   In general, employers are looking for two things: proof that a candidate can handle a specific job and (p. 633)
    a.   excellent references.
    b.   high employment test scores.
    c.   evidence that the person will fit in with the organization.
    d.   long-term commitment to the organization.

d _____ 7.   When it comes to drug and alcohol testing (p. 634)
    a.   by law only government agencies can require it.
    b.   some 45 percent of all companies now require it of all applicants.
    c.   the great majority of companies now require it.
    d.   the Supreme Court has declared it unconstitutional.

b _____ 8.   When asking questions during a job interview, you (p. 637)
    a.   stick to neutral topics such as the weather.
    b.   steer the discussion into areas where you can present your qualifications to peak advantage.
    c.   stick to questions that elicit simple yes or no answers.
    d.   put as much pressure on the interviewer as possible.

a _____ 9.   Which of the following is an example of an open-ended question that you might ask a job interviewer? (p. 638)
    a.   "How do you see your company improving its product sales in the next five years?"
    b.   "Have you already conducted many interviews for this job?"
    c.   "Does your company provide additional training?"
    d.   "How soon would the job start?"

a _____ 10.   When going in for a job interview, it's best to take (p. 639)
    a.   a list of questions to ask the interviewer.
    b.   some kind of object to occupy your hands, such as a pen or a key ring.
    c.   a tape recorder.
    d.   all of the above.

a _____ 11.   The best way to counteract feelings of shyness, self-consciousness, or nervousness about job interviews is to (p. 639)
    a.   identify and deal with the source of these feelings.
    b.   use humor to mask these feelings.
    c.   act overly confident to counteract these feelings.
    d.   see a psychotherapist, since you obviously can't deal with such a serious problem on your own.

b _____ 12. If you speak in a flat, emotionless tone during an interview, it will give the interviewer the impression that you are (p. 641)
   a. businesslike and professional.
   b. passive or bored.
   c. cool and at ease.
   d. sophisticated.

d _____ 13. When choosing the clothing you will wear for an interview, the best policy is to (p. 642)
   a. pick something that will make you stand out from the crowd.
   b. wear only dark colors.
   c. dress as you expect your interviewer to be dressed.
   d. dress conservatively.

a _____ 14. When going to a job interview, (pp. 642–643)
   a. take along samples of your work; recruiters are impressed by tangible evidence of job-related accomplishments.
   b. there is no need for you to bring copies of your résumé; you can assume the interviewer already has one.
   c. try not to be more than five or ten minutes late.
   d. do all of the above.

c _____ 15. If you are a smoker and must go to a job interview (p. 643)
   a. ask the interviewer politely if you can smoke.
   b. smoke only if the interviewer smokes.
   c. refrain from smoking.
   d. smoke just prior to the interview to calm yourself.

b _____ 16. Your goal in the initial screening interview is to (p. 643)
   a. explain your greatest strengths in depth.
   b. call attention to one key aspect of your qualifications.
   c. clinch the deal.
   d. show the interviewer that your personality fits well with the job.

b _____ 17. If you are asked back for a final job interview, the interviewer will most likely be concerned with (p. 644)
   a. your previous job experience.
   b. your personality.
   c. your educational background.
   d. checking your references.

a _____ 18. Most interviewers begin making a decision about the applicant (p. 644)
   a. within the first minute.
   b. during the question-and-answer stage.
   c. during the final minutes of the interview.
   d. after the candidate has left.

b _____ 19.   The longest phase of a job interview is (p. 644)
   a.   the warm-up.
   b.   the question-and-answer stage.
   c.   the close.
   d.   none; all are about the same length.

c _____ 20.   When a job interviewer indicates the interview is coming to a close, you (p. 646)
   a.   try to prolong the interview, since the more the interviewer interacts with you, the better impression you'll make.
   b.   leave as quickly as possible.
   c.   prepare to leave but try to pin down what will happen next.
   d.   ask how you did.

c _____ 21.   On your second or third visit to an organization, if you haven't been told by the end of an interview whether you got the job, you (p. 646)
   a.   don't bring up the topic.
   b.   mention that you have another job offer and need to give the other company an answer by a specific date.
   c.   ask tactfully when you can expect to learn of the decision.
   d.   ask whether you did anything wrong during the interview.

d _____ 22.   When you discuss salary requirements with a job recruiter, you (p. 646)
   a.   let the interviewer raise the topic first.
   b.   say that you expect to receive the standard salary for the job.
   c.   try to negotiate a higher salary if you are not satisfied with the offer and are in a good bargaining position.
   d.   do all of the above.

c _____ 23.   Within two days after an interview, you (p. 648)
   a.   have a friend call to see whether you got the job.
   b.   write a follow-up letter (using the format for persuasive messages) and include another copy of your résumé.
   c.   write a short note of thanks (using the format for routine messages).
   d.   assume that you didn't get the job if you haven't heard anything.

c _____ 24.   Use an inquiry letter as a follow-up to a job interview if you (p. 649)
   a.   would like to have more information about the job.
   b.   are running low on funds and really need the job.
   c.   have received a job offer from another firm and need to make a decision.
   d.   want to bring your name to the interviewer's attention once again.

a _____ 25.   Letters asking for time to consider other job offers follow the format for (p. 650)
   a.   direct requests.
   b.   bad-news messages.
   c.   persuasive messages.
   d.   goodwill messages.

b _____ 26.   When writing a letter accepting a job, keep in mind that (p. 651)
     a.   it begins with a buffer.
     b.   it constitutes a legally binding contract between you and the employer.
     c.   it is written within two weeks of receiving the job offer.
     d.   all of the above are true.

b _____ 27.   When writing a letter declining a job offer, you begin with (p. 651)
     a.   an apology.
     b.   a buffer.
     c.   a statement of the bad news.
     d.   a cheery greeting.

d _____ 28.   Which of the following letters would *not* follow the direct plan? (p. 651)
     a.   inquiry
     b.   request for time extension
     c.   letter of acceptance
     d.   letter declining a job offer

c _____ 29.   In a letter of resignation, you (p. 651)
     a.   follow the direct plan.
     b.   air your gripes with the organization.
     c.   state your intention to leave and the termination date.
     d.   do all of the above.

b _____ 30.   Which of the following letters would follow the bad-news plan? (p. 652)
     a.   letter accepting a job offer
     b.   letter of resignation
     c.   letter requesting a time extension
     d.   all the above

FILL-INS

1.   _____ _____ interviews, such as those on college campuses, are a
means of eliminating unqualified applicants. (p. 629)

2.   In a _____ interview, the job applicant meets with several interviewers who all ask
questions in a single session. (p. 630)

3.   In a _____ interview, the interviewer controls the situation by asking a series of
prepared questions in a set order. (p. 631)

4.   In a _____ interview, several candidates are interviewed simultaneously to see how
they interact. (p. 631)

5. In a _____ interview, the candidate is asked pointed questions designed to irk or unsettle him or her. (p. 631)

6. In a _____ interview, candidates are asked how they would handle real-life work problems. (p. 632)

7. Job applicants with a high _____ tend to be high in self-awareness, have good impulse control, and are persistent, confident, and self-motivated. (pp. 632–633)

8. You are more likely to be invited back for a second job interview if your _____ signals convince the interviewer that you are alert, assertive, confident, and responsible. (p. 641)

9. Following a job interview, send a _____ note even if you feel you have little chance of landing the job. (p. 648)

10. If you haven't heard from an employer within two weeks after an interview, send a letter of _____. (p. 649)

11. If you receive a job offer but are waiting to hear from other possible employers, request a _____ _____. (p. 649)

12. A letter accepting a job offer follows the _____ plan. (p. 650)

13. A letter declining a job offer follows the _____ plan. (p. 651)

14. A letter of resignation follows the _____ plan (p. 652)

ANSWERS

1.	preliminary screening	8.	nonverbal
2.	panel	9.	thank-you
3.	structured	10.	inquiry
4.	group	11.	time extension
5.	stress	12.	good-news
6.	situational	13.	bad-news
7.	EQ	14.	positive

COMPONENT CHAPTER A
FORMAT AND LAYOUT OF BUSINESS DOCUMENTS

TRUE OR FALSE

T _____ 1. The design for letterhead stationery should be as simple as possible. (p. 660)

T _____ 2. The standard line length in a normal business letter is about 6 inches. (p. 661)

F _____ 3. In business documents, dashes are typed as space, hyphen, space. (p. 661)

F _____ 4. "Sept. 10th, 1999" is the correct way to type the date in a letter. (p. 663)

T _____ 5. If you are writing a business letter to someone you know well, it is acceptable to use his or her first name in the salutation. (p. 666)

T _____ 6. Three blank lines are left between the complimentary close and the sender's typed name. (p. 667)

T _____ 7. The second page of a letter includes a heading containing the name of the person or organization receiving the letter, the page number, and the date. (p. 668)

F _____ 8. Mailing information, such as "Special Delivery" or "Registered Mail," is typed on the envelope instead of the letter. (p. 670)

F _____ 9. In the simplified letter format, commas follow both the salutation and the complimentary close. (p. 670)

T _____ 10. Most envelopes used in business are No. 10 (9 1/2 inches long). (p. 674)

T _____ 11. The U.S. Postal Service abbreviations for Alabama, Alaska, Arizona, and Arkansas are AL, AK, AZ, and AR, respectively. (p. 675)

F _____ 12. A memo has a complimentary close and a signature. (p. 677)

F _____ 13. E-mail messages can act as memos but not as letters. (p. 678)

F _____ 14. All meetings, no matter what size, have a formal printed agenda that is distributed to all participants well in advance of the meeting. (p. 683)

T _____ 15. The minutes of a meeting include the times at which the meeting started and ended, all major decisions reached, summaries of important discussions, and a list of all who were present. (p. 684)

MULTIPLE CHOICE

b _____ 1. The quality of paper is measured by (p. 660)
    a. length and width.
    b. weight and cotton content.
    c. color and texture.
    d. whether or not it is imprinted with the name and address of the company.

a _____ 2. The proper sequence for the standard parts of a letter is (p. 661)
    a. heading, date, inside address, salutation, body, complimentary close, signature block.
    b. date, heading, inside address, salutation, body, typewritten name, complimentary close.
    c. salutation, date, heading, inside address, body, complimentary close, signature block.
    d. inside address, heading, date, salutation, body, complimentary close, typewritten name.

c _____ 3. Which of the following is a salutopening? (pp. 690–666)
    a. Dear Professor Milford:
    b. Dear Esteemed Professor Milford,
    c. Thank you, Professor Milford,
    d. Attention: Professor J. J. Milford

d _____ 4. You may place the attention line (p. 667)
    a. at the top of the page, centered under the letterhead.
    b. below the salutation.
    c. two lines below the complimentary close.
    d. on the first line of the inside address.

d _____ 5. What is the correct format for reference initials? (p. 670)
    a. RSR/sm
    b. RSR:sm
    c. RSR:SM
    d. all of the above

a _____ 6. The letter format in which all parts begin at the left margin is called (p. 670)
    a. block.
    b. modified block.
    c. simplified.
    d. mixed.

b _____ 7. To meet the needs of U.S. postal equipment, envelopes (p. 675)
    a. are never made of colored paper.
    b. are addressed in capital letters, with no punctuation.
    c. include all mailing instructions below the address area.
    d. adhere to all of the above guidelines.

a _____ 8. The top of a memo usually includes headings for (p. 677)
  a. date, to, from, subject.
  b. department, date, subject.
  c. attention, to, from, date.
  d. subject, to, date.

c _____ 9. The chief advantage of a memo-letter is that (p. 680)
  a. it is lighter than a regular letter and therefore can be mailed more cheaply.
  b. no inside address is required.
  c. it eliminates the need for addressing the envelope.
  d. it can be sent electronically.

c _____ 10. When preparing a formal report, (p. 682)
  a. leave a uniform 2-inch margin on all sides.
  b. leave a 2-inch margin at the top and bottom and a 1-inch margin on the sides.
  c. leave a 1-inch margin on three sides and a 1-1/2-inch margin on the bound side.
  d. leave a uniform 1-1/2-inch margin on all sides.

COMPONENT CHAPTER B
DOCUMENTATION OF REPORT SOURCES

TRUE OR FALSE

F _____ 1. Always use APA style for documentation in your reports, even if your employer or client normally uses a different form. (p. 686)

F _____ 2. The *Chicago* style refers to the documentation style used by companies in the Chicago area. (p. 686)

T _____ 3. In the humanities system, bibliographic citations are given in either footnotes or endnotes. (p. 686)

T _____ 4. Footnotes and endnotes are identical; the only difference between the two is their placement. (p. 686)

T _____ 5. The humanities system relies on superscript numbers to let readers know how to look for a footnote or endnote. (p. 687)

F _____ 6. Content notes are used to document quotations and paraphrased passages. (p. 687)

F _____ 7. The only format difference between endnotes and a bibliography is that the bibliography is in alphabetical order. (p. 687)

F _____ 8. If a newspaper article doesn't have an author, your citation begins with the name of the newspaper. (p. 687)

F _____ 9. If you use unpublished materials, such as doctoral dissertations or public speeches, as resources, you do not need to cite them in your report. (p. 687)

T _____ 10. The American Psychological Association style uses the author-date system. (p. 688)

T _____ 11. The *APA* style recommends listing as references only those works actually cited in the text. (p. 688)

T _____ 12. In References prepared following *APA* style, the date of publication comes immediately after the author's name. (p. 688)

F _____ 13. In the *APA* style, titles of articles are put in quotation marks and all important words are capitalized. (p. 691)

T _____ 14. If you use the *MLA* style, your in-text citations include the author's last name and a page reference within parentheses. (p. 691)

F _____ 15. With the *MLA* approach, you hold off compiling the Works Cited list until the rest of your report is completed. (p. 691)

MULTIPLE CHOICE

c _____ 1. With *Chicago*'s humanities style, you use (pp. 686–687)
a. the author-date system.
b. the author–page number system.
c. superscripts and footnotes or endnotes.
d. full citations within the text itself.

d _____ 2. The purpose of a superscript in text is to let the reader know (p. 687)
a. to read the marked line more carefully.
b. how many sources the author consulted.
c. that the report is scholarly.
d. to look for source information either in a footnote or an endnote.

a _____ 3. A content note (p. 687)
a. offers additional information or provides a cross-reference.
b. documents direct quotes.
c. documents paraphrased passages.
d. documents visual aids.

c _____ 4. With the *Chicago* style, the Bibliography (p. 687)
a. lists only those works actually cited in the text.
b. lists works in the order in which they were cited in the text.
c. can include annotations.
d. all of the above.

a _____ 5. Entries for the Bibliography for a report following the *Chicago* style (p. 687)
a. use quotation marks around the titles of articles from newspapers and journals.
b. alphabetize magazine articles by the name of the magazine if no author is cited.
c. capitalize only the first words of titles of books and articles.
d. use only the name of the principal author, followed by "et al." to represent any other authors.

a _____ 6. With the *APA* style, you use (p. 688)
a. the author-date system.
b. the author–page number system.
c. superscripts and footnotes or endnotes.
d. full citations within the text itself.

c _____ 7. When preparing the list of references following the *APA* style (pp. 690–691)
   a. include all the works you consulted, even if you didn't actually cite them anywhere in the text.
   b. include full information on any personal communications or interviews you conducted in your research.
   c. use the title "References."
   d. do all of the above.

b _____ 8. With the MLA style, you use (p. 691)
   a. the author-date system.
   b. the author–page number system.
   c. superscripts and footnotes or endnotes.
   d. full citations within the text itself.

d _____ 9. In the List of Works Cited following the *MLA* style (pp. 691–692)
   a. the date comes immediately after the author's name.
   b. electronic sources are not included.
   c. the titles of books and periodicals are put in quotation marks.
   d. all the main words are capitalized in the titles of books and articles.

b _____ 10. When citing journal articles using the A*PA* style (p. 692)
   a. use quotation marks around the title.
   b. capitalize only the first word of the title and the first word to follow an internal colon.
   c. you do not need to include the volume number.
   d. include only the first page of the article.

APPENDIX I
FUNDAMENTALS OF GRAMMAR AND USAGE

TRUE OR FALSE

T _____ 1. The plural of "son-in-law" is "sons-in-law," but the possessive is "son-in-law's." (p. A2)

T _____ 2. The pronoun "who" is in the nominative case; the pronoun "whom" is in the objective case. (p. A3)

F _____ 3. The verb "do" is an example of a regular verb. (p. A5)

T _____ 4. The difference between "lie" and "lay" is that "lie" is an intransitive verb and "lay" is a transitive verb. (p. A5)

T _____ 5. Many adverbs are formed by adding "ly" to adjectives. (p. A7)

F _____ 6. A phrase is made up of a group of words that includes both a subject and a predicate. (p. A8)

F _____ 7. A comma splice is the use of a comma and a coordinating conjunction to separate two independent clauses. (p. 19)

T _____ 8. A linking verb is always followed by a noun, pronoun, or adjective. (p. A10)

T _____ 9. A semicolon is used to separate independent clauses when the second one begins with a word such as "however" or "therefore." (p. A11)

T _____ 10. You need not include a comma when a date consists only of the month and year. (p. A12)

F _____ 11. A period goes inside quotation marks if the whole sentence is quoted but outside the quotation marks if only the last part of the sentence is a quote. (p. A13)

F _____ 12. If you need to divide the word *sincerely* at the end of a line, you divide it at the *ly*. (p. A15)

T _____ 13. A common mistake is to write "alot" instead of "a lot." (p. A17)

T _____ 14. A writer implies; a reader, in seeing between the lines, infers. (p. A17)

F _____ 15. There are no mispelled words in this sentence. (p. A17)

MULTIPLE CHOICE

b _____ 1.   Which of the following is the most gender-neutral (and correct) sentence? (p. A3)
a.   A manager must use his best judgment.
b.   Each department head must hire her or his own staff.
c.   Every shopper will be issued her own personal credit card.
d.   Each technician has their own tool kit.

d _____ 2.   Which of the following possessive phrases is *not* correct? (p. A4)
a.   a year's recommendations
b.   two years' recommendations
c.   its recommendations
d.   it's recommendations

b _____ 3.   What is the tense of the verb in this sentence? "We issued the policy Monday afternoon." (p. A4)
a.   present
b.   past
c.   future
d.   past perfect

c _____ 4.   Which of the following words is an adjective? (p. A6)
a.   too
b.   silently
c.   poor
d.   badly

d _____ 5.   Which of the following is *not* a complete sentence? (pp. A7–A8)
a.   The bigger they come, the harder they fall.
b.   Put it in the mail right away.
c.   Come here.
d.   Depending on the circumstances.

a _____ 6.   What is the problem with this sentence? "We can give him a small raise, he deserves it." (p. A9)
a.   comma splice
b.   sentence fragment
c.   dangling modifier
d.   nothing

c _____ 7.   Which of the following punctuation marks is used to separate a dependent clause at the beginning of a sentence from the rest of the sentence? (p. A12)
a.   semicolon
b.   colon
c.   comma
d.   dash

a _____ 8. Which of the following terms should *not* be hyphenated? (p. A13)
    a. non-union
    b. pro-Republican
    c. self-assured
    d. ex-wife

d _____ 9. In the following sentence, which words should *not* be capitalized? "After talking with President Hilda Bruckner, he decided that the Insurance industry would provide a suitable career for someone who was a Graduate of the Department of Business at Gable University." (p. A14)
    a. insurance, department
    b. president, university
    c. graduate, department
    d. insurance, graduate

a _____ 10. Which of the following words is misspelled? (pp. A17–A18)
    a. accomodate
    b. exaggerate
    c. occurrence
    d. receive